KE-MA-HA

Ke-ma-ha

THE OMAHA STORIES OF

Francis La Flesche

EDITED BY
James W. Parins & Daniel F. Littlefield Jr.

University of Nebraska Press
LINCOLN & LONDON

© 1995 by the University of Nebraska Press
All rights reserved
Manufactured in the United States of America

♾ The paper in this book meets the minimum requirements of American
National Standard for Information Sciences — Permanence of Paper for
Printed Library Materials, ANSI Z39.48-1984.

Library of Congress Cataloging-in-Publication Data
La Flesche, Francis, d. 1932.
    Ke-ma-ha : the Omaha stories of Francis La Flesche / edited by
James W. Parins and Daniel F. Littlefield, Jr.
        p.   cm.
    Includes bibliographical references (p.   ).
    ISBN 0-8032-2910-0 (alk. paper)
    1. Omaha Indians — Fiction.   I. Parins, James W.   II. Littlefield,
Daniel F.
PS3523.A268K46   1995
813'.52 — dc20   94-9362
                                                              CIP

Contents

Introduction

THIS OFFERING OF EIGHTEEN stories — most published here for the first time — is the work of a talented and prolific writer and notable Omaha personage, Francis La Flesche. It is an attempt to follow through on his own plan — to bring a body of literature about his people to public attention. Published materials about or by the Omahas are scarce. While some ethnographical accounts of Omaha stories and tales have been published, most appear in scholarly tracts, and few attempts until now have been made to bring these works to the general public.[1] La Flesche's stories tell us a great deal about Omaha culture in ways that anthropological treatises cannot. Many are full of humor and deal with everyday human situations. He gives us an idea of what it was like to be growing up in his people's traditional culture before large influxes of white Americans changed that life forever. He presents as well retellings of tales that were preserved in the Omaha folk tradition since time immemorial. Here, too, are found fictional accounts of the coming together of the white and Indian cultures on the western plains and of how they often clashed.

All in all, these stories are an important and unique body of writing that establishes La Flesche's place in the American Indian literary tradition. In recent years, the works of Charles A. Eastman (Santee), Zitkala-Ša (Yankton), and Alex Posey (Creek) have been republished, and critical attention has been turned to Sophie Alice Callahan (Creek), John Oskison (Cherokee), and other writers. With the publication of this volume, concepts of both the variety and richness of the literature written by American Indians near the turn of the century should be expanded. La Flesche was distinct among those writers in the range of his production, and this volume offers insight, we believe, into his versatility. Though scholars apparently have known about La Flesche's unpublished short fiction for some time, their concern with him has been biographical or has emphasized his role as an ethnologist. This collection of short fiction, together with his monumental ethnographic works and his slightly fictionalized autobiography, *The Middle Five* (1900), make him the most prolific, the most versatile, and, therefore, perhaps the most important Indian writer of the period.

La Flesche was born on the Omaha Reservation in present northeastern Nebraska in 1857, only a few years after it had been established and the Omahas had begun a major change in their society. Though La Flesche's half-French father, Joseph La Flesche, or Estamaza (Iron Eye), was instrumental in pressing Omaha assimilation, as a child and youth the younger La Flesche apparently participated in the ceremonial life of the Omahas and in three buffalo hunts, including the last that the Omahas made. Joseph La Flesche concluded that his children must live in a far different world from his and made sure that they had a modicum of education. Susette (1854–1903), Rosalie (1861–1900), Marguerite (1862–1945), and Susan (1865–1915) — his daughters by Mary Gale — attended local schools, and all but Rosalie went east for additional schooling. Francis (1857–1932), Lucy (1865–1923), and Cary (1872–1952) — Joseph's children by Ta-in-ne — attended local schools; only Lucy went east for further study. Francis's only formal education in his early years was obtained during the 1860s, when he attended for a time the Presbyterian mission school on the reservation. During this time he learned English, in which he ultimately reached a fluency that made him one of the Omahas' best interpreters.[2]

Omaha society underwent considerable stress in the 1870s. As the buffalo disappeared, the ceremonial life that was dependent on it declined. Many Omahas were attempting to make a transition to Christianity and to farming. In addition, there were concerns about the validity of their land title. Their concerns were intensified in 1878 when the neighboring Poncas were removed to the Indian Territory. The return of Standing Bear and some of his Ponca followers to Nebraska in 1879 brought the first public attention to Francis La Flesche. In 1879 and 1880, he traveled throughout the East as a chaperon for his sister Susette ("Bright Eyes"), who accompanied Standing Bear and Thomas H. Tibbles as they sought to stir public sentiment in behalf of Standing Bear's displaced Poncas, who were attempting to regain their homelands. Their efforts created a news sensation and brought considerable attention not only to the Ponca cause but to Standing Bear's entourage. In 1881 La Flesche was appointed to the Bureau of Indian Affairs, where he was copyist and, later, clerk until 1910. The move from the reservation was significant, for it put him in Washington, virtually at the center of ethnographic studies in America. Yet he did not sever ties with the reservation but spent his summer vacations there and at other times involved himself with tribal affairs by mail.[3]

In 1882 there began a close relationship between Alice Fletcher and La Flesche that lasted until her death in 1923. At the time, Fletcher was a budding ethnographer with close ties to Harvard's Peabody Museum in Cambridge, Massachusetts. Through Susette, whom she had met during the Standing Bear tour, she became involved in the Omaha allotment issue and in the spring of 1882 traveled to Washington to lobby for passage of an allotment bill. Though she had also met Francis La Flesche during his eastern tour, their friendship did not begin until she conferred with him in Washington and they discovered common interests in ethnology. La Flesche had been introduced to the formal study of Omaha ethnology and linguistics by James Owen Dorsey, who began his work among the Omahas in 1878. La Flesche translated for his father, who was one of Dorsey's main informants. La Flesche himself contributed to Dorsey's *Omaha Sociology* (1884) and was at times at odds with his father and other informants concerning Omaha practices. In addition, he gave Dorsey a number of stories, which appear in Dorsey's *The Ɔegiha Language* (1890) along with those contributed by Joseph, Mary Gale, and Susan La Flesche. At Dorsey's suggestion, La Flesche also attempted to collect and record the songs related to the Omaha Sacred Pole ceremony but did not get far with his study.

When Fletcher was appointed allotting agent for the Omahas in 1883, he was sent with her as her interpreter. After allotment was finished in 1884, he assisted her in the field and collected information and translated for her during her work with the Omahas. A bond of affection developed between the two, which Fletcher described as that of a mother and son. She informally adopted La Flesche in 1891, and they made their home together in Washington from then until her death. Fletcher taught him the methods of ethnographic research as they pursued the study of the Omahas together, and he became her invaluable assistant because of his linguistic, cultural, and musical understanding and skills. With La Flesche's help, Fletcher — his friend, companion, adopted mother, and mentor — established herself as a recognized scientist in ethnology. Meanwhile, he published articles on death and funeral customs of the Omahas and on Omaha buffalo medicine men, and received credit, upon publication, for his assistance in Dorsey's linguistic study and Fletcher's study of Omaha music. In addition, La Flesche earned the L.L.B. degree in 1892 and the L.L.M. a year later from the National University.[4] In years that followed, he used his legal expertise to assist delegations from various tribes as they pursued their business with the federal bureaucracy. By 1899, La Flesche was known for not only his ethnographic and linguistic skills but also in the East and in Washington social circles as the adopted son and protégé of Alice Fletcher.

At that time, he was preparing a collection of slightly fictionalized narratives about his childhood experiences in mission school on the Omaha Reservation. The book was a radical departure from the ethnographic study and writing for which La

Flesche, now middle-aged, was known. In early June of 1899 La Flesche submitted the manuscript of what would become *The Middle Five: Indian Schoolboys of the Omaha Tribe* to the editors at Doubleday and McClure Company, who rejected it. Although they liked it, they were concerned about reader reaction; judging the popular tastes of the day, they believed readers would expect something about the "wilder" aspects of Indian life. La Flesche's stories about Indian boys at school, wrote Doubleday editor H. W. Lanier, could with few exceptions be about *any* boys, and he asked La Flesche to consider expanding the volume to appease the reading public. "It does not seem to us," Lanier said, "that the school life should necessarily be excluded, but certainly the burden should be thrown upon the other *wilder* existence." If La Flesche would rewrite following this suggestion, Lanier was sure that he could produce "something which would really show the outside world what the life of the Indians actually was and is."[5] La Flesche requested that his manuscript be returned "express." Lanier complied, but persisted by urging La Flesche once more to consider writing "something which would show the actual life of the Indian in his wilder state."[6]

At this point, Alice Fletcher intervened as she often did to open avenues of success for La Flesche. She gave his manuscript to Bliss Carman, the popular poet and former editor for *The Independent*, who read it, liked it, and forwarded it with an endorsement to Herbert Small of the Boston publishing house of Small, Maynard and Company. By the middle of August, Small had offered to publish *The Middle Five* and had begun making suggestions for revisions.[7]

When Lanier learned about the arrangement with Small, he was not surprised. He felt certain that the publisher "would more than come out even" in the venture. Doubleday and McClure would have published it, he said, if they could have been assured of a "moderate success," but what the company really wanted was "a great big thing," something about the "wild life" that "would make a stir." Through a mutual acquaintance, Lanier learned that La Flesche planned to write such a book. He believed that the McClure Company could probably offer La Flesche an advance on "a book like that"[8] because it "could hardly fail of success" and wrote La Flesche that he hoped to see all or part of a manuscript before long.[9]

At a time when boys' literature was extremely popular, Lanier wanted to capitalize on the public's knowledge of La Flesche. He wrote, "Any one who picked up a volume written by you about Indian boys would, I think, naturally expect to get from it a more intimate picture of Indian life than he had before been able to secure. I know this is what I expected and wanted, and I think that it is just in the difference between the life of the Indian boys and the life of other boys that you could make your work so superior to that of any one else, from your better knowledge."[10]

Whether La Flesche had contemplated writing a volume of stories before Lanier suggested it, he was probably doing so by the time Bliss Carman recommended his manuscript to Small, Maynard and Company. He was certainly doing so by the middle of October 1899. When Lanier congratulated him on the contract with Small, Maynard and Company, La Flesche responded immediately with an offer to go to New York to discuss the second book with him. Lanier was enthusiastic, believing that La Flesche's "special knowledge and ability" and the "absolute novelty" and "interest" inherent in the subject would allow them to produce a book "that would stand as the first authoritative picture of the real Indian boy and which would be extremely popular."[11] Whether La Flesche had any manuscript at this time is uncertain, for he laid the proposed project aside in order to revise the manuscript of *The Middle Five*. On November 26, Alice Fletcher noted in her diary: "F. began Ke ma ha, goes well."[12]

In January 1900, La Flesche was at work on "Ke-ma-ha," as he called his book, when Zitkala-Ša's "Impressions of an Indian Childhood" appeared in the *Atlantic Monthly*. Small believed that her work would be useful in "handling" *The Middle Five* "by helping to create an interest in the general subject."[13] Lanier, however, wrote La Flesche with some urgency. Though Zitkala-Ša's work dealt with Indian girlhood, it appeared that she had cut into the market that Lanier had hoped to reach; while he did not believe that her work would make a difference in the success of La Flesche's collection of stories concerning boys, he stressed the importance of moving forward as quickly as possible and asked for manuscript. La Flesche apparently promised to have something to show Lanier by early February; Lanier pressed, suggesting that his book might fit well into Doubleday's Boys' Library series.[14] Meanwhile, La Flesche had heard that the Macmillan Company was looking for a volume of stories "from an Indian point of view." Perhaps Lanier pressed too hard, or perhaps La Flesche was simply testing the market, for he sent Macmillan a single story, implying that he had others that he planned to publish as a volume. Kate Stephens, a company representative, asked for the other stories to consider, for Macmillan could not make an agreement to publish without seeing the whole manuscript.[15]

La Flesche then turned back to Lanier. La Flesche was a petulent sort and perhaps did not like Stephens's rejection. Or perhaps he did not like something in her response; Macmillan, it seems, was interested in "legends" that were "simply told" as someone by a fireside might tell to children. The best comparison that she could make was to the Uncle Remus stories, those "lovely legends of the darkies."[16] Though there are elements of the storytelling frame in some of his stories, that kind of story was not necessarily what La Flesche had in mind. Also, he probably did not have enough finished manuscript to send Stephens, for in early March he offered a single story — probably the one that he had sent to Macmillan — to Lanier. Lanier now said, however, that there was no need to hurry the manuscript; his enthusiasm had apparently cooled somewhat. "Whenever you do get ready," he wrote, "please remember we shall take the greatest interest in reading 'Ke-ma-ha.' " Correspondence between the two ceased until early July, when Lanier wrote that he had heard "by accident" that La Flesche had "about finished" his "book on the Wild Life of an Indian Boy" and that he looked forward to seeing the manuscript.[17]

That the project was that far along seems unlikely though La Flesche was at work on the stories during the summer of 1900. In late July he wrote his brother-in-law Edward Farley that he was just completing a story for the *Southern Workman*, published at Hampton Institute. This story, "The Laughing Bird," which he had worked on during January, is probably the one that he had sent to Macmillan and had offered to Lanier. After it was accepted, he sought assurances from the *Workman* that the story was protected by copyright and that he had permission to reprint it in his collection of stories, which he indicated was about finished.[18]

During the next few months, La Flesche continued his fiction writing. In late September Fletcher sent James Murie, her Pawnee informant and fieldworker, a copy of *The Middle Five* with La Flesche's compliments, excusing him for not writing himself by saying that he was "very busy writing stories and planning another book."[19] In November, La Flesche wrote his nephew Caryl that he was "busy working on some short stories for a paper in Boston," and he apparently continued writing fiction into early 1901. By then he had finished and submitted one story and was at work on another. In late January 1901 he sent "The Buffalo Ride," the first of his known stories from this period to have Kema-ha as a character, to the *Youth's Companion*, which did not publish it. "The Story of a Vision" appeared in the *Southern Workman* in February. Early that month, Fletcher wrote that La Flesche's workload had been so heavy at the Bureau of Indian Affairs during the winter that he had little energy for writing in the spring, and by the following summer he was apparently writing little.[20] By then, he had also likely abandoned the idea of a collection of stories about Omaha boys.

Several reasons are possible for La Flesche's abandonment of his attempts at a literary career. First, about the time Lanier's enthusiasm for the project cooled, Doubleday and McClure broke up, the former becoming Doubleday, Page and Company and the latter becoming McClure, Phillips and Company in January 1900. In 1902 McClure brought out Charles A. Eastman's *Indian Boyhood*, which did in autobiography what Doubleday and McClure had tried to get La Flesche to do in fiction three years earlier. During 1900 and 1901, when La Flesche was most thoroughly engaged in the project, he saw Eastman socially on occasion.[21] It may be that he knew of Eastman's plans for a book about his childhood; or perhaps Eastman's plans emerged after La Flesche had given up his. At any rate, the appearance of *Indian Boyhood* made it less likely that another press would be much interested in publishing a book on the same subject.

Second, his ambitions for the project fed off the excitement surrounding his placing *The Middle Five* with a publisher. That book was supposed to have launched his literary career. Zitkala-Ša wrote him shortly after it appeared in the summer of 1900: "Here is just a whiff of wind from the Dakota prairie to whisper in your very heart 'Bravo!' " and she concluded, "At this distance I rejoice in your success."[22] Richard H. Pratt, founder of the Carlisle Indian school, told La Flesche that the book had made him cry, and he encouraged La Flesche to write a sequel about a lone boy off the reservation, which he thought would be particularly instructional for boys. One reviewer wrote that "in their purpose and movement these stories have the wholesome quality of naturalness that marks them as among the best of their kind. In this respect the reader is frequently reminded of that prince among juvenile books, T. B. Aldrich's 'Story of a Bad Boy.'

Although the two books differ widely in detail, they are alike in the simplicity and truthfulness with which they reveal The Boy."[23] Though it caused a brief sensation as a new book by "an Indian" and was widely reviewed, mainly in newspapers, real success did not follow. When Small, Maynard and Company sent La Flesche's first royalty check in early 1901, they reported "steady" sales and "good reviews," but the check was small. This report coincided with the marked decrease in his fiction writing in 1901. Though Small, Maynard and Company had financial difficulties in 1902, the company survived, and when the stock of *The Middle Five* was depleted in 1906, the publisher wanted to print a school edition. Apparently dissatisfied with his royalties, and perhaps believing that an inexpensive edition lessened the value of his work, La Flesche refused.[24]

Third, the idea of a literary career for La Flesche may have resulted from a "family" spat between him and Fletcher. According to Joan Mark, Fletcher's biographer, their relationship reached one of its crisis points in 1898 as a result of an unspoken but certain desire on La Flesche's part to have more public acknowledgment of his contributions to her ethnographic work. It was important to her, too, that he achieve honor and fame. Since their relationship had begun in the early 1880s, there had been periods when gossip concerning it had been particularly vicious; yet she had weathered those times, made a name for herself, and earned renown and acceptance in the scientific world of ethnology and archaeology. La Flesche needed to find his place. However, Fletcher was reluctant to share her professional limelight with him. Thus, according to Mark, it was probably by mutual consent that they went their own ways; a literary career for La Flesche, she argues, "seemed the near-perfect solution to an otherwise intractable if unspoken problem. Alice Fletcher did not want to share her scientific reputation with Francis La Flesche, but he was no longer willing to remain in the background."[25]

Fletcher actively sought to help him launch his literary career. In November 1898, they read from their respective works-in-progress before the Folklore Society of Baltimore, he from *The Middle Five* and she from a popularization of some of her ethnographic work, *Indian Story and Song from North America*.[26] When Doubleday rejected his manuscript of *The Middle Five* in late spring 1899, she sent it to Bliss Carman; not hearing from Carman quickly enough, she contacted a publisher in Chicago and directed La Flesche to visit him on his way back from a trip to Nebraska. When Carman recommended the manuscript and Small, Maynard and Company offered to publish it, she fed La Flesche's self-confidence. "You can write," she told him, "and if you will keep at it, you can make for yourself a name in letters, that is, in literature." Her faith in his literary ability was being confirmed, and she urged him to take his "place among writers," make his name "one of honor," and win "the happiness and fame" he deserved.[27]

Fletcher continued to manipulate matters while attempting to make it appear to be La Flesche's affair. When Carman suggested that she write an introduction for *The Middle Five*, she wanted someone in "the world of letters" to write it, perhaps Carman or Charles Dudley Warner, whom she would ask.

When Small asked her to write an introduction, she suggested to him that La Flesche write a preface. Her excuse was that she stood "for Science, rather than Letters,"[28] but more important, it must not appear that it was her influence that got him published. She had a long conference with Herbert Small in his offices early in September, and she, not La Flesche, sent him the preface on October 10. She helped La Flesche put the preface in final form and also apparently took a hand in revising the manuscript. As soon as the revision was completed, La Flesche began work in earnest on "Ke-ma-ha." Fletcher played a less conspicuous role in his efforts to publish this projected volume of short stories, though she kept friends and acquaintances apprised of his ongoing literary activities.[29]

Perhaps the most significant reason La Flesche abandoned his proposed collection of short stories was that he lacked the intensity of literary skill or was unwilling to commit the time necessary to do it. Though Fletcher insisted that he had the makings of a writer, she warned him that writing was hard work. Devoted to her as he was, he gave it an honest effort. His manuscripts reveal a strong sense of possibilities for narratives and reflect his attempts at extensive revision, sometimes complete rewriting. In the summer of 1900, Fletcher gave Emily S. Cook, assistant to the commissioner of Indian affairs, a copy of La Flesche's story that had been accepted for the *Southern Workman*. Cook was "much pleased with the beginning, and in fact with all," though she thought the two-thousand-word limit set by the *Workman* had "hurried the latter part to its detriment." She recognized the "keen joy" Fletcher was experiencing through his success and pondered what the future held for La Flesche "in a literary sense."[30]

Whether she realized it or not, Cook had put her finger on the problem with much of La Flesche's fiction. It was not the two-thousand-word limit that was at fault but La Flesche himself. His literary leavings are full of brilliant beginnings, bright flashes of language, and narrative fits and starts that rarely move to climax or conclusion. Having generated as many fictional fragments as he did, La Flesche must have recognized his limitations. It is perhaps well that he did and determined not to invest much time in fiction writing. Though Fletcher tried to involve him in playwriting and he later collaborated on the libretto for an opera, he ultimately gave up on a literary career. He resumed collaboration with Fletcher in her work on the Omahas.[31] That collaboration, in turn, prepared him for his own work on the Osages, which he began after he was transferred from the Bureau of Indian Affairs to the Bureau of American Ethnology in 1910. The Osage research, along with his earlier work with Fletcher on the Omahas, would establish his place as an ethnologist.[32]

Overall, La Flesche's fiction stands like an unwritten chapter of his autobiography. Based to a large extent on the life he knew before he went to the mission school, it describes a time lost forever. The gulf between that earlier life and the present stood in sharp relief to him in the summer of 1895 when he made his annual visit to the Omaha country, this time taking with him a graphophone, the new sound-recording device with which he intended to capture Omaha songs. For his "comfort and pleasure," he said, he set up a tent to live in. "The last days of my real tent life," he later wrote, "came to an end years ago when I with other Indians traveled one whole winter through western Kansas in search of buffalo. At that time my proud possessions were a saddle, a bridle, a lariat and a gun. In singular contrast to those things, I had with me in my temporary 'return to the tent' a number of books, magazines, a leather case and a graphophone." The changes in his life paralleled changes in Omaha life in general: "The great herds that my people and I followed over the plains in the days of my youth have gone the same way that my forefathers have gone never to return. The songs that expressed the emotions of my people, the songs of war, of peace and of love that used to ring through the wooded hills of my birth were also passing away and it was to catch as much as possible the dying echoes that I made my visit home armed with a speech and song catching instrument. The tent was a bit of sentiment, the indulgence of which the civilized people will forgive."[33] His fiction, like *The Middle Five*, is written recordings of the "dying echoes" of his earlier life. It is significant that in his first draft of this statement he had written that the great herds and his forefathers "live only in story," which he revised to read "have gone never to return."

This attitude toward Omaha culture, expressed only three or four years before the launching of his literary career, had been shaped in large measure by his association with Alice Fletcher. She had been a strong advocate for breaking up the reservations through allotment of lands in severalty and for assimilation of Indians into American society. She had been instrumental in shaping the provisions of the General Allotment Act, popularly known as the Dawes Act, of 1887 and had served as allotting agent for the Omaha, Winnebago, and Nez Perce reservations. As a scientist, she had been interested in recording the "dying echoes" of Indian cultures for study, in which endeavor La Flesche had been a key figure. He had worked diligently in the field, collecting information and material objects. He had even laid the groundwork for her acquisition, as museum specimens, of the Sacred Pole and other sacred objects most revered by the Omahas. By 1900, however, Fletcher's attitude toward Indian cultures had shifted dramatically, according to Joan Mark, her biographer. Fletcher had seen the devastating results of allotment and concluded that assimilationist policies had failed. Despite those policies, cultures persisted. She no longer believed that Indian life ways should be replaced by Western ones, but that much in them should be "conserved."[34]

As went Fletcher, so went La Flesche. In the 1880s, he, like the other members of his family, had been a strong supporter of allotment for the Omahas. However, by 1900 his support had eroded. At the Lake Mohonk Conference, an annual gathering of reformers at Lake Mohonk, New York, he described how allotment theory had failed in practice for his people.[35] His life as a career bureaucrat at the Bureau of Indian Affairs should have taught him that, if nothing else. But he had personal knowledge as well. His family had split along factional lines that rent the Omahas after allotment.[36] If, like Fletcher, he now acknowledged that allotment had failed and that native cultures should be "conserved," his enthusiasm for the fictional rendering of a time in Omaha history that was "never to return" might have faded in light of his growing sense of urgency to record and "conserve" what still existed.

Though we cannot from this distance say with certainty what La Flesche intended in his proposed volume, we might gain some insights from examining his concerns regarding *The Middle Five*. When, in rejecting the manuscript, H. W. Lanier said he could detect no differences between the Omaha boys and *any* boys except in certain instances, he had hit upon one of La Flesche's basic intentions in the book: La Flesche had wanted to show that Indian boys had much in common with others. He had chosen to write about his schoolfellows instead of "his other boy friends who knew only the aboriginal life . . . not because the influences of the school alter the qualities of the boys, but that they might appear under conditions and in an attire familiar to the reader." La Flesche wrote, "The paint, feathers, robes, and other articles that make up the dress of the Indian, are marks of savagery to the European, and he who wears them, however appropriate or significant they might be to himself, finds it difficult to lay claim to a share in common human nature. So while the school uniform did not change those who wore it, in this instance, it may help these little Indians to be judged, as are other boys, by what they say and do."[37] He told Bliss Carman, "I have been anxious to have the little stories in the book come to light with the hope that the intelligent class of white people will get a better understanding of the character of the people of my race." Carman's recommendation that the manuscript be published had given him, he said, the "courage to go on with other work which I have been planning."[38] This, presumably, was the collection of stories about boys before the days of mission school, and we might assume that he intended it as a complement to his earlier volume.

In his preface to *The Middle Five*, La Flesche projected himself and his companions who make up the characters of the book back to a time before their school experience. He reflects on their birth in the aboriginal dwellings of the Omaha people, their passage through the cradleboard stage, and their liberation from the cradleboards that allowed them, he said, "to get into all sorts of mischief as we explored the new and wonderful world in which we found ourselves."[39] As they explored that world, they learned to conform to the demands of Omaha social courtesies and etiquette, acquired a correct use of the Omaha language, and developed the fondness of their people for companionship, conversation, and games.[40] From the descriptions of La Flesche's projected volume of short fiction, we can safely assume that this was the world that he wanted to depict in that second work. His literary leavings help to confirm that assumption, for they offer, in completed stories and fragments, myriad glimpses of boyhood experiences in an earlier time in Omaha society, and many of them center on the themes he reflected upon in the preface to *The Middle Five*.

Though we cannot now reconstruct La Flesche's projected volume, we can, once more, make some reasonable assumptions. We can name, for instance, three stories that he worked on during 1900 and early 1901, when he was at work most intensely on the project: "The Laughing Bird, the Wren: An Indian Legend," "The Story of a Vision," and "A Buffalo Ride." He inquired about reprinting the first, and in the last, Ke-ma-ha, whose name La Flesche had offered as the title of his projected volume, appears as a character. There can be little doubt that he intended to include these stories in the collection. La Flesche's literary corpus includes, besides these, fifty-odd pieces of fiction in completed stories and fragments. What his intentions were for these remaining pieces is uncertain.

A majority of the stories reflect La Flesche's strong sense of an intended audience: the youthful reader. He makes that audience clear in his plans for the collection as a companion to *The Middle Five*, his correspondence with prospective publishers, and the places he sought to publish, such as the *Southern Workman* and *Youth's Companion*. He might well have inscribed the collection to the same reader as that to whom he inscribed *The Middle Five:* "To The Universal Boy." Thus the stories offer a glimpse into Omaha life, but not to show the "wild" life of Omaha boys as Lanier had wanted him to do. There are, to be sure, some scenes — of warfare and ceremonials, for instance — that appealed to the romantic imaginations of white readers who believed that the Indians were vanishing. Far more typical, however, are vignettes of daily life: hardships, danger, family bonds, social etiquette, moral growth, mischief, and humor.

The completed but unpublished stories fall into three loose categories based on subject. Most concern boyhood and early youth: "A Buffalo Ride," "A Buffalo Hunt," "A Discovery and an Experience," "Kae-zhin-ga," "Tae-hon'-zhon," "Wa-ha-ton-ga," "Ta-de'-win," and "The Captive Maid." In these stories boys appear as characters or as listeners to old men who recount episodes of their earlier lives, often their childhood or their youth. The published stories, "The Laughing Bird" and "The Story of a Vision," also fall into this category. A second group are, for the most part, renditions of traditionally told Omaha narratives: "The Twins and Two-Face," "The Spring, the Mischief Maker, and the Tree," "He-ba-cha-ge and Sin-de-dum-pa," and "Kae-tun-ga on the War Path." And a third group of stories deal with the more recent past and the reservation period: "A Ghost Story," "Hal Baker," "Ne-ma-ha," and "Marion, the Book Vendor, and I."

In the first group, the tales of boyhood, La Flesche seems to be attempting to reach his white audience with the message that Indian boys are like other boys. It is their common humanity that is important, not the fact that one wears a buffalo robe, the point he tried to make in *The Middle Five* and intended to continue in his companion volume. His young characters play games, make mild mischief, emulate and admire older boys and men, and conspire against parental authority just as their white counterparts do.

It seems equally clear that in the stories of boyhood and in the traditional tales, La Flesche was promoting the value of conserving traditional culture. He tries to show that there is a worth in Omaha culture that goes beyond white society's appreciation of aboriginal behavior that appears unusual by Euro-American standards. The culture has inherent value. It contains aspects generally admired by human beings: what others would call patriotism; appreciation of personal acts of bravery; regard for elders, love of children, and other close familial ties; respect for nature; and a sense of a spiritual life that transcends the material, among other things. It follows that a culture that values these most human of traits must be worth "conserving," to use Fletcher's term, and should not be obliterated through misguided policy, thoughtless action, or deliberate acts motivated by greed.

The stories in the second group, though based largely on traditional tales, are not ethnographic tracts. Yet Omaha ethnography is part of the fabric of many of them. In "The Twins and Two-Face," for instance, La Flesche drops some episodes from the traditional tale recorded by Dorsey (1890) and adds new ones. "He-ba-cha-ge and Sin-de-dum-pa" and "Kae-tun-ga on the War Path" are versions of stories recorded by Dorsey. Always, however, there is evidence that La Flesche was aware of his audience. He streamlined the narratives, eliminating or glossing some passages or episodes and reducing the repetitions common in oral performances. In doing so, La Flesche exhibits some of his best skills as a fiction writer.

The third group of stories, those that deal with the Omaha country after the arrival of the whites and during the period in which the Indians were being encouraged to put aside their traditional ways, are overall less successful. The largest portion of unfinished manuscript among La Flesche's papers and stories involves Robert Redwing. In these works, La Flesche seems to be exploring the thematic possibilities of assimilation. A regular cast of characters appears, led by the protagonist, Redwing (or, alternately, Merriman), who has been raised as a traditional

Omaha, but who is later adopted by loving white parents. Robert makes the transition between the Omaha and white worlds easily, using all the outdoor skills he learned as a boy to his advantage in his new life, excelling in his studies at the best schools, and adapting painlessly to the world of business and commerce. He is generous, honest, open, and helpful and in general makes his adopted parents proud. It is inevitable that the lovely young white daughter of the Indian agent, faced with such a blend of nobility, intellect, ability, and masculinity, falls in love with Robert. In "A Story," the longest unfinished manuscript, for instance, the beautiful young heroine, Dorothy, quite naturally enough, finds it impossible not to fall in love with him. One evening under the stars, Redwing tells her how as a boy he saved the life of a prominent white man, who promptly adopted him and enrolled him in a college in Lexington, Kentucky. "It was the beginning of my training in the manners of the civilized," Robert says in the last sentence of the unfinished story. Here, and in all the Redwing fragments, once the process of Robert's assimilation into white society seems complete, the tales abruptly end. La Flesche seems unable to do anything else with his characters or his plot. It is as if there is nothing else to say, unless it is that the road to assimilation leads nowhere.

La Flesche did finish one story on this theme, "Ne-ma-ha." Ne-ma-ha is a young lad whose cruel father banishes him to fend for himself on the lonesome prairie. After he prays for delivery from his precarious situation, two white men run across the boy seemingly by accident. He is adopted by one of the men, a rich New Orleans–based merchant, and grows up to be a paragon of virtue, strength, intelligence, and virility in true Redwing fashion. However, when Ne-ma-ha returns to his homeland as a young man, he recognizes his mother and is reunited with her. As the story ends, Ne-ma-ha, formerly Robert Merriman, walks arm in arm with his mother toward the lodges and into the dawn.

La Flesche obviously had a personal interest in the assimilation theme he tries to work with in the Redwing stories. He had enjoyed a traditional Omaha childhood, but it was one spent in a time of transition for his people. It was early in his lifetime that the buffalo disappeared from the prairies, the reservation was broken up, and the Omahas were assigned their individual landholdings. He entered the white world in 1881 and stayed there except for his ethnographical expeditions and family visits. And there is ample evidence that he enjoyed his life and work in white society; his diaries tell of frequent visits to the opera and theater, of social evenings within a circle of friends, and regular dinners and lunches with colleagues. But he must have had a sense of displacement, too. In Washington, he often acted as middleman, as he had done for Fletcher during the Omaha allotment, meeting with delegations from Indian country, interpreting, often mediating. He represented individual Indians in their business with the Indian Bureau, often having to explain the Indian's point of view to white bureaucrats and the white man's rules and procedures to the Indian. In addition, La Flesche never reached the pinnacle of success in the "civilized" society to which he aspired and toward which his white friends urged him. He was to remain in Fletcher's shadow as an ethnographer until her death, and his literary career faltered early.

La Flesche's revisions indicate that he wrote fiction with difficulty, and the condition of his manuscripts suggests that he never
arrived at a literary style that satisfied him. As a reader, singer,
and avid theatergoer who had worked closely with Fletcher and
who, like her, viewed ethnography as a science, La Flesche knew
the difference between the precise, denotative language of science and the connotative, figurative language of literature. Moving from one to the other may have been the source of some of
his problems in writing. His task in fiction was different, even,
from the writing of *The Middle Five*. That work was autobiography, slightly fictionalized. In fiction, on the other hand, he had to
create scene, character, and action; even when he relied on
traditional narratives, he had to adapt those for modern readers.
The laboriousness of his literary effort might explain his lack
of success with the popular press, in which he published little.
He simply got little of it ready to send out. Though Norma Kidd
Green says that he published a number of stories in obscure
newspapers and magazines, she offers no evidence.[41] His diaries
and correspondence indicate that he sent a few stories out, but
if they were published, they have not been located. Perhaps
his lack of confidence or success with literary forms resulted
from work habits derived from long years of ethnological work,
closely observing, recording detail, transcribing songs, and making musical notations, all slow, time-consuming tasks.

He certainly felt a frustration a few years later as he attempted
to find a happy medium between ethnological science and literature during his collaboration with Nelle Richmond Eberhart on
the libretto for the opera "Da-o-ma." La Flesche proposed the

opera in the fall of 1908. He and Fletcher had become interested in the work of Charles Wakefield Cadman, an ambitious young composer whose current efforts involved music based on Fletcher's studies of Omaha music. Eberhart had supplied the lyrics for Cadman's *Four American Indian Songs*. She agreed to write a libretto for the opera based on a story by La Flesche, and Cadman agreed to orchestrate it.[42] For the story, La Flesche fell back on an outline for a five-act play that he had written in March 1900 in collaboration with Fletcher and Mabel Barrows. The story line of the proposed play, "Ka-wa-ha's Love Song," was adapted from two unfinished stories, "Ka-e-la's Love Song" and "Ka-wa-ha's Love Song." In the story, Ni-da-we follows her lover, Ka-wa-ha, into the field to fight the enemy. They are married just before the battle, during which Ka-wa-ha is betrayed into the enemy's hands by his jealous friend, A-de-ton, who hopes to win Ni-da-we. She refuses to retreat with A-de-ton, but follows her husband to the enemy's camp and rescues him from captivity. They return to their village, and A-de-ton flees. La Flesche retained the story line, with minor changes, in "Da-o-ma," which he originally titled "Daoma and Adeta." In it, the characters are Sioux, not Omaha. Ae-de-ta and Ne-ma-ha are rivals for the love of Da-o-ma; in the end, however, Ne-ma-ha does not escape but kills himself.[43]

For the next four years, La Flesche worked not only with Eberhart on the libretto but with Cadman on selection of Omaha music to adapt to the story. His relationships with them were sometimes stormy, La Flesche concluding at times that Cadman knew too little about Indian music and that Eberhart took too much license with ethnography. On their parts, they concluded that La Flesche knew too little about operatic forms, and Eberhart occasionally reminded him condescendingly of the ways in which stylized conventions of the opera conflicted with "real life."[44] But La Flesche knew the opera, having attended many productions through the years. Apparently his devotion to ethnographic science prevented his taking the fictional license with his subject that his collaborators felt was necessary.

Had La Flesche's literary skill been equal to that of other Indian writers of his era, his attitude toward native cultures after 1901, when he put fiction writing aside, would probably have prevented his joining their ranks. Writers such as Charles A. Eastman, Carlos Montezuma, Zitkala-Ša, and others associated with the Society of American Indians dominated the Indian literary scene during the next twenty years. They were politically active, strongly advocating Indians' adoption of Anglo-American values as the best course under the circumstances, elimination of the reservation system, suppression of the use of peyote, and dissolution of the Bureau of Indian Affairs.[45] Like those writers, La Flesche attended the first conference of the Society of American Indians in 1911, but he caused resentment in some participants when he argued not only that the reservations should be preserved but that the society should hold its meetings there and seek input from the rank-and-file Indians.[46] Though usually labeled a "progressive," La Flesche no longer believed in a political solution to culture crisis. Assimilation, like allotment, was more easily argued theoretically in the popular press than made a reality in everyday Indian life. He believed that Indians, like others in America, should be left to live as they pleased and, unlike most of his contemporary Indian writers, ultimately stood on the side of the Native American Church.[47] He left politics to others and continued his ethnological work.

La Flesche's position, though no doubt influenced by Fletcher, resulted in part from twenty-five years of ethnological fieldwork and constant contact with reservation Indians. He had returned to the Omaha country regularly during his summer vacations and sought out the older Omahas. At the time the Society of American Indians was founded, he was in Oklahoma engaged in fieldwork among the Osages. Even in Washington his contact with reservation Indians continued. From the time he arrived there in 1881, he sought out Indian delegations who came to the city and visited them at their hotels or brought them home with him. Unlike most of his educated Indian contemporaries, he did not urge the Indians to forget the old ways, but patiently coaxed, cajoled, even bribed them to remember, and he found that they remembered much, quite often more than they were willing to tell.

After 1901, then, La Flesche turned from the aspects of Indian life that were "never to return," aspects that he had sought to describe in his fiction. He once more turned his attention to those that persisted and helped to rescue much of Omaha and Osage ritual, ceremony, song, and language from oblivion. His efforts at establishing a literary career, embodied in *The Middle Five* and in his short fiction, represent only an interlude in the development of a remarkable Omaha intellect.

Here, for the first time, the best of his short fiction is collected. The copy texts consist of two published and sixteen unpublished stories. "The Laughing Bird" and "The Story of a Vision" appeared in the *Southern Workman*. The unpublished stories were selected from fifty-four manuscript items labeled "La Flesche's Literary Attempts" in the Alice C. Fletcher collection at the Smithsonian's National Anthropological Archives. Among those items are typescript and holograph manuscripts of fictional pieces, autobiographical recollections, the libretto for "Da-o-ma," and the plot summary for the five-act play, "Ka-wa-ha's Love Song."

In editing the manuscript stories, we have corrected obvious typographical errors and misspellings; we have also made changes in La Flesche's punctuation to make it conform more closely to current standards and have regularized variant spellings and the use of hyphens within individual stories. However, in an effort to preserve La Flesche's style we have made no substantive changes.

To assist the reader with ethnographic matters, we have taken the following editorial steps. We have provided each story with a headnote containing commentary on ethnographic matters and definitions of terms relevant to the narrative. Esoteric matters that cannot be treated effectively in headnotes are presented in endnotes. Definitions, commentary, or name identifications that can be inserted unobtrusively in the text appear in brackets. For assistance with ethnographic matters, we have consulted Fletcher and La Flesche, *The Omaha Tribe*, and Dorsey, *Omaha Sociology* and *The Ȼegiha Language*. We have made no attempt to translate personal names, for in instances where names take on significance in the story, La Flesche either defines them or makes their meanings clear in context. We have retained La Flesche's stress marks and phonetic/syllabic spellings of names and terms in the texts of the stories, a system he apparently adopted to accommodate the general reader. However, for the spelling of Omaha names or terms in headnotes or footnotes, we have adopted the system of Fletcher and La Flesche,[48] whose phonetic guide is as follows:

> All vowels have the continental values.
> Superior n (^{n}) gives a nasal modification to the vowel immediately preceding.
> x represents the rough sound of h in the German *hoch*.
> *th* has the sound of *th* in *the*.
> *ç* has the sound of *th* in *thin*.
> Every syllable ends in a vowel or in nasal n (^{n}).

ACKNOWLEDGMENTS

We thank the staff of the National Anthropological Archives, Smithsonian Institution, not only for their ready assistance with the La Flesche materials but also for their permission to reprint the stories. We also thank the staff of the Nebraska State Historical Society for making the La Flesche family papers available to us. Finally, we thank the University of Arkansas at Little Rock for a faculty research grant to Daniel F. Littlefield Jr., which provided major support for this work.

NOTES

1. A large body of traditional stories and other narratives appears in James Owen Dorsey, *The Ɔegiha Language*, Smithsonian Institution, Bureau of Ethnology, Contributions to North American Ethnology, 6 (Washington, D.C.: Government Printing Office, 1890). A popular edition of Omaha literature is Paul A. Olson, ed., *The Book of the Omaha: Literature of the Omaha People* (Lincoln: Nebraska Curriculum Development Center, 1979),

2. Norma Kidd Green, *Iron Eye's Family: The Children of Joseph La Flesche* (Lincoln: Johnsen Publishing Co., 1969), 42–50.

3. Green, *Iron Eye's Family*, 52–53, 64–66; Joan Mark, *A Stranger in Her Native Land: Alice Fletcher and the American Indians* (Lincoln: University of Nebraska Press, 1988), 38, 47. Though a number of sources touch on the biography of La Flesche, Mark's biography of Fletcher offers the best insights into the life of La Flesche because of its extended treatment of his life and career. Other sources include Hartley B. Alexander, "Francis La Flesche," *American Anthropologist* 35 (1933): 328–31; Green, *Iron Eye's Family*, especially chapters 3 and 8; Margot Liberty, "Francis La Flesche: The Osage Odyssey," in Liberty, ed., *American Indian Intellectuals* (St. Paul: West, 1978), 44–59; Liberty, "Native American Informants: The Contribution of Francis La Flesche," in John V. Murra, ed., *American Anthropology: The Early Years* (St. Paul: West, 1978), 99–110; Michael C. Coleman, "The Mission Education of Francis La Flesche: An American Indian Response to the Presbyterian Boarding School in the 1860s," *American Studies in Scandinavia* 18 (1986): 67–82.

4. Mark, *A Stranger in Her Native Land*, 70–79, 86–95, 219–22; La Flesche, "Death and Funeral Customs among the Omahas," *Journal of American Folk-Lore* 2 (October 1889): 3–11; La Flesche, "Omaha Buffalo Medicine-Men, and Two Songs Sung at an Operation," *Journal of American Folk-Lore* 3 (July 1890): 215–21; James Owen Dorsey, *Omaha Sociology*, Third Annual Report of the Bureau of American Ethnology, 1881–82 (Washington, D.C.: Government Printing Office, 1884); Alice C. Fletcher, *A Study of Omaha Indian Music* (Cambridge, Mass.: Peabody Museum of American Archaeology and Ethnology, 1893). For an analysis of discrepancies between La Flesche's and others' interpretations of Omaha ethnology, see R. H. Barnes, *Two Crows Denies It: A History of Controversy in Omaha Sociology* (Lincoln: University of Nebraska Press, 1984).

5. H. W. Lanier to Francis La Flesche, June 10, 1899, La Flesche Correspondence, Alice C. Fletcher Papers, National Anthropological Archives, Smithsonian Institution. This collection is hereafter cited as Fletcher Papers.

6. Lanier to La Flesche, June 13, 1899, La Flesche Correspondence, Fletcher Papers.

7. Bliss Carman to Miss Fletcher, August 10, 1899; La Flesche to Carman, n.d.; Herbert Small to Madam [Fletcher], August 16, 1899; and Small to La Flesche, August 23 and 28, 1899, La Flesche Correspondence, Fletcher Papers.

8. Theodore Waters to La Flesche, October 16, 1899, La Flesche Correspondence, Fletcher Papers.

9. Lanier to La Flesche, October 14, 1899, La Flesche Correspondence, Fletcher Papers.

10. Lanier to La Flesche, June 10, 1899, La Flesche Correspondence, Fletcher Papers.

11. Lanier to La Flesche, October 24, 1899, La Flesche Correspondence, Fletcher Papers.

12. Entries for November 19 and 26, 1899, Alice C. Fletcher Diaries, Fletcher Papers.

13. Small to La Flesche, February 23, 1900, La Flesche Correspondence, Fletcher Papers.

14. Lanier to La Flesche, February 9, 1900, La Flesche Correspondence, Fletcher Papers.

15. Kate Stephens to La Flesche, January 17, 1900, La Flesche Correspondence, Fletcher Papers.

16. Stephens to La Flesche, January 17, 1900, La Flesche Correspondence, Fletcher Papers.

17. Lanier to La Flesche, March 9 and July 3, 1900, La Flesche Correspondence, Fletcher Papers.

18. Entries for January 3 and 8, July 1, and August 22, 1900, La Flesche Diaries; William L. Brown to La Flesche, August 18, 1900, La Flesche Correspondence, Fletcher Papers; La Flesche to Ed Farley, July 23, 1900, La Flesche Family Papers (MS 2026), Nebraska State Historical Society. The last collection is hereafter cited as La Flesche Family Papers.

19. Alice C. Fletcher to James Murie, September 27, 1900, Fletcher Correspondence, Fletcher Papers.

20. La Flesche to Caryl, November 25, 1900, La Flesche Family Papers;

entries for January 6, 13, and 21, and February 7 and 10, 1901, La Flesche Diaries, Fletcher Papers; Mark, *A Stranger in Her Native Land*, 277; entry for January 21, 1901, Fletcher Diary, Fletcher Papers.

21. Entries for May 22, 1900, and January 24 and 25, 1901, La Flesche Diaries; entry for February 21, 1901, Fletcher Diary, Fletcher Papers.

22. Zitkala-Ša to La Flesche, August 10, 1900, La Flesche Correspondence, Fletcher Papers.

23. R. H. Pratt to La Flesche, September 17, 1900, Personal Letters re "The Middle Five," Fletcher Papers; "Book Reviews," *Southern Workman* 29 (October 1900): 581.

24. John Miley to La Flesche, February 20, 1901, La Flesche Correspondence, and C. L. Stebbins to La Flesche, October 6, 1906, and February 26 and March 11, 1907, Personal Letters re "The Middle Five," Fletcher Papers; Green, *Iron Eye's Family*, 191.

25. Mark, *A Stranger in Her Native Land*, 263–64, 273–74.

26. Mark, *A Stranger in Her Native Land*, 274.

27. Entries for June 12 and 22, July 6 and 10, and August 5, 6, and 8, 1899, Fletcher Diaries; Fletcher to La Flesche, July 29, August 14, and August 19, 1899, Fletcher Correspondence, Fletcher Papers.

28. Fletcher to La Flesche, August 14 and 19, 1899, Fletcher Correspondence, Fletcher Papers.

29. Emily S. Cook to Fletcher, August 10, 1900, La Flesche Correspondence; Fletcher to Murie, September 27, 1900, Fletcher Correspondence; and entries for September 5 and 25, October 10, and November 19, 1900, Fletcher Diaries, Fletcher Papers. Fletcher's stamp on La Flesche's preface is clear. Among his story fragments in the Fletcher Papers is a holograph labeled "Whirlwinds," written on the back of part of his holograph of the preface for *The Middle Five*. Revisions are in Fletcher's handwriting.

30. Cook to Fletcher, August 10, 1900, Fletcher Correspondence, Fletcher Papers.

31. Mark, *A Stranger in Her Native Land*, 293.

32. For La Flesche's career as an ethnologist, see Liberty, "Francis La Flesche: The Osage Odyssey"; Liberty, "Native American Informants"; and Joan Mark, "Francis La Flesche: The American Indian as Anthropologist," *Isis* 73 (1982): 497–510.

33. La Flesche, "The Song of Flying-Crow," La Flesche's Literary Attempts, Fletcher Papers.

34. Mark, *A Stranger in Her Native Land*, 265–69.

35. Isabel C. Barrows, ed., *Proceedings of the Eighteenth Annual Meeting of the Lake Mohonk Conference of Friends of the Indian, 1900* (n.p.: The Lake Mohonk Conference, 1901), 76–78.

36. Green, *Iron Eye's Family*, 82–121.

37. La Flesche, *The Middle Five: Indian Schoolboys of the Omaha Tribe* (1900; reprint, Lincoln: University of Nebraska Press, 1978), xv.

38. La Flesche to Carman, n.d., La Flesche Correspondence, Fletcher Papers.

39. La Flesche, *The Middle Five*, xvi.

40. La Flesche, *The Middle Five*, xvi–xvii.

41. Green, *Iron Eye's Children*, 189.

42. Charles Cadman to La Flesche, December 4, 1908, La Flesche Family Papers; Cadman, *Four American Indian Songs* (New York: White-Smith Music Publishing Company, 1909).

43. The unfinished stories and the outline of "Ka-wa-ha's Love Song: An Indian Play in Five Acts" as well as the libretto of "Da-o-ma" are in the file labeled "La Flesche's Literary Attempts," Fletcher Papers. A fragment of "Daoma and Adeta, a Dakota Story" and La Flesche's revised libretto for "Da-o-ma" are in the La Flesche Family Papers.

44. La Flesche's relationship with Cadman is described in detail in Harry D. Perison, "Charles Wakefield Cadman: His Life and Works" (Ph.D. diss., University of Rochester, 1978), especially 95–119. For his relationship with Eberhart, see particularly Eberhart to La Flesche, May 20 and 24, August 8, and October 17, 1909, and April 27, 1910; Cadman to La Flesche, May 4 and June 29, 1910, La Flesche Family Papers.

45. For a recent analysis of the political milieu in which Eastman, Montezuma, Zitkala-Ša, and other Indian writers worked, see Robert Allen Warrior, "Reading American Indian Intellectual Traditions," *World Literature Today* 66 (Spring 1992): 236–40.

46. La Flesche to Fletcher, October 9, 1912, La Flesche Correspondence, Fletcher Papers.

47. Entries for February 21, 22, and 25, and March 5 and 7, 1918, La Flesche Diaries, Fletcher Papers.

48. Fletcher and La Flesche, *The Omaha Tribe* (1911; reprint, Lincoln: University of Nebraska Press, 1992), 28. Here we follow the lead of R. H. Barnes, who points out that their orthography "is by far the easiest to print" (xiii).

Part One

Stories of Boyhood and Youth

The Laughing Bird, the Wren:
An Indian Legend

The story of the wren contained in the following narrative is the old narrator's retelling of "The Bird Chief," a story that Francis La Flesche told to the ethnologist James Owen Dorsey, who was engaged in fieldwork among the Omahas from 1878 to 1881. This version contains a hint of the traditional beliefs concerning some birds, such as the swallows that heralded the approach of storms and of Thunder, the war god. However, despite the title, the story of the wren is no more important than the fictional framework in which La Flesche places it. He uses the framework to provide insight into the storytelling scene: the circular earthen lodge with its domed roof and willow furnishings, the crackling fire, and the intimacy it creates between the teller and his listeners. It also reflects the rapport between the old man and the boys: their eager anticipation, their respect for the teller, and his mild but firm control of the scene. Finally, the humorous episode of the hapless dog reinforces La Flesche's assertion in The Middle Five *and elsewhere that children learned the lessons of etiquette early in life, in this case not to pass between the host and the fire. This story was published in the* Southern Workman *29 (October 1900): 554–56.*

J A-BAE-KA CAME IN WITH A BIG armful of wood, threw it down with a crash, stamped his feet, and gave his blanket a few vigorous flaps to shake off the snow. The squint-eyed little chap was always willing to go after water or wood or to run on any other errand, and when a thing of that kind was to be

3

done, the dozen boys who were chums and went together always looked to him first.

A dozen hands were stretched to place the wood on the fire, and a number of mouths were blowing upon it. Soon the flames leaped upward with a roaring, crackling noise, and the sparks chased each other in a lively fashion up through the round opening at the top of the dome-shaped roof on the earth lodge. The light threw a ruddy glare upon our youthful faces, and our shadows danced in a fantastic manner against the somber walls of the large, circular room.

"Wha! Goo'-da-ga!" exclaimed a black-eyed youngster as he gave a whack with the back of his hand to the little spotted dog that came smelling and sniffing in front of our venerable story teller, who sat filling his pipe and staring into the flames to refresh his memory. The little dog gave a yelp and quickly disappeared under one of the willow compartments in the back part. Even little dogs were required to show respect to story tellers.

The old man lifted his small pipe stem upward toward the sky and muttered a few words; then every boy quickly bent forward, each one eager to be first to hold the brand for the story teller to light his pipe. After taking a few whiffs, the venerable man began, and all of us youngsters fell to an attentive silence.

"Of all the living things brought into existence by the breath of Wa-kon'-da,"[1] remarked the old man by way of introduction, "none but the birds possess the wonderful power of leaving the earth, lifting themselves into the air, and moving at will in the midst of the restless winds.

"Once in the progress of time, so the story tellers say, there came out of the ever silent depths of the blue, far above the reach of earthly sounds, a mysterious voice commanding the feathered creatures of the earth to gather at a certain place, where on an appointed day they were to display their power of flight.

"In obedience to this command all the birds hastened toward the chosen spot, some flying in flocks; some speeding along in lines; others soaring alone; each according to the habit of its kind. From the lakes, the rivers, and the marshes came the geese, the ducks, the gulls, and all the birds that find their food in the waters; out of the black forests emerged the vultures, the hawks, the owls, the crows, and the magpies; from the sandhills came the cranes whose loud calls, resembling the cry of a warrior, could be heard from river to river; from the sandy banks of the streams and from the rocky cliffs came the swallows, the messengers of cloud and storm; from the 'Four Winds,' from any and every direction came birds large and small with plumage of varied hue, each one intent on having a share in the coming contest.

"The shadow of night passed westward over the hills and valleys, and 'the great star' [morning star, or Venus] appeared, heralding the grey dawn of the appointed day. When the first rays of the sun shot upward, myriads of voices were lifted to give to the great day a joyous welcome. Then, as though touched by a common impulse, every wing in that vast multitude was stretched, and each bird, uttering its mystic cry, put forth its strength and rose for the momentous struggle. As the thousands upon thousands of wings whipped the air, an awe-inspiring sound, like to an angry tempest plunging through a forest of gigantic pines, vibrated over the land, and the earth became darkened by countless shadows as the confused mass of birds sped swiftly toward the sky.

"On the limb of a dead oak sat an eagle smoothing the feathers of his wings with his hooked beak as though indifferent to the struggles that were going on about him. Among the whitened branches of the same tree a little brown bird moved about in a restless manner, at times almost touching the eagle but unnoticed by him. At length the huge bird spread his great wings, gave a powerful spring, and mounted the air with wild cries. The lifeless tree quivered from the shock, and from its branches the decaying bark fell piece by piece to the ground. With a few vigorous strokes the eagle gained his poise and was soon soaring upward with increasing speed in ever widening circles, seemingly without effort and as though borne aloft by the wind alone.

"At the moment the eagle had lifted his wings for flight the little brown bird had darted under one of them, fixed its tiny claws in the feathers, and buried itself in the soft down close to the body of the mighty bird. There it clung safe from the violence of the wind while the eagle, all unconscious of his burden, swept onward. He passed the meadow lark already descending to the earth having given up the race, but nonetheless happy and filling the air with the sweetest of melodies. The curlew, the thrush, the robin, and other small birds were also fluttering earthward, each singing its own song, content with this power although outflown in the race by the larger birds.

"The eagle with the little brown bird under his wing quickly passed the slow-moving crow and the raven; overtook the swift hawk; further on he swept by the forked-tail kite, who among all the winged creatures is unequaled in grace and beauty; then he distanced the crane; and at last he passed the buzzard, the grandfather of all birds. Still the eagle went on, rising higher and higher, until the trees, then the hills, and at last the high mountains flattened to a level, and the earth itself began to grow dim.

"The struggle was over; no living thing met the eye of the weary eagle as he gazed into the empty space around him. All at once he felt a strange stir under his wing, as with a sudden whirr out flew the little brown bird from its cover, filling the air with a mischievous song as it darted about. Then, laughing as it sped upward, it soared away into the sunlight, leaving the astonished eagle far below.

"For the merry wit by which the little brown bird won the honors of that great day, it was given the name Ki'-ha-ha-ja, laughing bird.

"You have all heard the laughter of that little bird. He builds his nest in hollow trees, and when the leaves are out in the spring, he fills the woods with delightful sounds. No bird is happier than he. Shae-ton."

"Woo-hoo!" we all exclaimed in chorus. "What a beautiful story."

"But it's so short, Grandfather," said Ne-ne'-ba, who was always wanting more. "Tell us another one."

"Yes!" we all echoed. "Tell us another one, Grandfather."

"No, little ones. Go now to your homes," replied the aged

man. "And dream of that tiny, laughing bird who cheated the great eagle out of his victory."

At last we reluctantly arose, took our leave of the old man, and made for the doorway, leaving him sitting there cleaning his pipe, his face radiant with a kindly smile. As we passed through the long entrance way of the lodge, we pushed each other and scuffled with boyish laughter, and when we came out into the open air, we drew our blankets over our heads and raced for our own lodges through the falling snow.

NOTE

1. "It is difficult to formulate the native idea expressed in this word. The European mind demands a kind of intellectual crystalization of conceptions, which is not essential to the Omaha, and which when attempted is apt to modify the original meaning. Wako[n]'da stands for the mysterious life power permeating all natural forms and forces and all phases of man's conscious life." Fletcher and La Flesche, *The Omaha Tribe*, 597.

The Story of a Vision

The framework of this story, the second in a sequence, continues La Flesche's emphasis on the winter setting for storytelling in the earthen lodge and contains one of his frequent reminders of Omaha etiquette, learned early in childhood. The story of the vision contained inside the narrative framework suggests the rarity of murder among the people in earlier times and provides an occasion for the old storyteller to reflect on the changes that have occurred in their society during his lifetime when he says, in reference to the strange events surrounding the vision, that now the Omahas "are getting to be different." This story was published in the Southern Workman *30 (February 1901): 106–9.*

E ACH OF US, AS WE GATHERED AT the lodge of our story teller at dusk, picked up an armful of wood and entered. The old man who was sitting alone, his wife having gone on a visit, welcomed us with a pleasant word as we threw the wood down by the fire-place and busied ourselves rekindling the fire.

Ja-bae-ka and Ne-ne-ba, having nothing to do at this moment, fell to scuffling. "You will be fighting if you keep on," warned the old man.

"Stop your fooling and come and sit down," scolded Wa-du-pa. "You're not in your own house."

The flames livened up cheerily and cast a ruddy glow about us when Wa-du-pa said, "Grandfather, the last time we were here you told us the myth of the eagle and the wren; we like it, but now we want a true story, something that really happened, something you saw yourself."

"How thirsty I am!" said the old man irrelevantly. "I wonder what makes me so dry."

"Quick!" said Wa-du-pa, motioning to Ja-bae-ka. "Get some water!"

The lad peered into one kettle, squinted into another, and then said, "There isn't any."

"Then go, get some!" arose a number of voices.

"Why don't some of you go?" Ja-bae-ka retorted, picking up one of the kettles.

"Take both!" someone shouted.

Ja-bae-ka approached the door grumbling. As he grasped the heavy skin portiere to make his way out, he turned and said, "Don't begin until I come back."

We soon heard his heavy breathing in the long entrance way. "It's moonlight, just like day!" he exclaimed, as he set the kettles down and thrust his cold hands into the flames with a twisting motion. "The boys and girls are having lots of fun sliding on the ice."

"Let them slide, we don't care!" ejaculated Wa-du-pa as he dipped a cup into the water and handed it to the old man, who put it to his lips and made a gulping sound as he drank, the lump in his throat leaping up and down at each swallow. At the last draught he expelled his pent-up breath with something like a groan, set the cup down, wiped his lips with the back of his hand, and asked, "A real true story—something that I saw myself; that's what you want, is it?"

"Yes, Grandfather," we sang out in chorus. "A story that has you in it!"

His face brightened with a smile, and he broke into a gentle laugh, nodding his head to its rhythm.

After a few moments' musing, and when we boys had settled down, the old man began: "Many, many winters ago, long before any of you were born, our people went on a winter hunt, away out among the sand hills where even now we sometimes go. There was a misunderstanding between the leaders, so that just as we reached the hunting grounds, the tribe separated into two parties, each going in a different direction.

"The weather was pleasant enough while on the journey, but a few days after the departure of our friends a heavy storm came upon us. For days and nights the wind howled and roared, threatening to carry away our tents, and the snow fell thick and fast, so that we could not see an arm's length; it was waist deep and yet it kept falling. No hunting could be done; food grew scarcer and scarcer, and the older people became alarmed.

"One afternoon as my father, mother, and I were sitting in our tent eating from our last kettle of corn, there came a lull, and we heard with startling distinctness a man singing a song of augury. We paused to listen, but the wind swept down again and drowned the voice.

" 'A holy man seeking for a sign,' said my father. 'Son, go and hear if he will give us words of courage.'

"My father was lame and could not go himself, so I waded through the heavy drifts and with much difficulty reached the man's tent, where many were already gathered to hear the predictions. I held my breath in awe as I heard the holy man say:

" 'For a moment the wind ceased to blow, the clouds parted, and in the rift I saw standing, in mid-air against the blue sky, the spirit of the man who was murdered last summer. His head was bowed in grief and although he spoke not, I know from the vision that the anger of the storm gods was moved against us for not punishing the murderer. Silently the spirit lifted an arm and pointed beyond the hills. Then I found that I too was in mid-air. I looked over the hilltops and beheld a forest where shadowy forms like those of large animals moved among the trees. I turned once more to the spirit, but the clouds had come together again.

" 'Before dawn to-morrow the storm will pass away. Then let the runners go to the forest that I saw and tell us whether or not there is truth in the words that I have spoken.'

"As predicted, the wind ceased to blow and the snow to fall. Runners were hastily sent to the forest, and the sun was hardly risen when one of them returned with the good news that the shadowy forms the holy man had seen were truly those of buffalo.

"The effect of the news upon the camp was like magic. Faces brightened, the gloomy forebodings that clouded the minds of the older people fled as did the storm, and laughter and pleasantries enlivened the place. The hunters and boys were soon plodding through the snow toward the forest, and before dark every one returned heavily laden, tired and hungry, but nonetheless happy. The fires burned brightly that night, and men told stories until it was nearly morning.

"The forest of the vision was a bag of game; every few days

the hunters went there and returned with buffalo, elk, or deer, so that even the poorest man had plenty for his wife and children to eat.

"All this time nothing had been heard from the party that separated from us before the storm. One night when I came home from a rabbit hunt, I found my mother and father packing up pemmican and jerked meat as though for a journey. I looked inquiringly at the pack as I ate my supper; by and by my mother told me that a man had just come from the other camp with the news that the people had exhausted their supplies, and as they could find no game, they were suffering for want of food. My sister and her husband were in that camp, and I was told to carry the pack to them.

"My father had arranged with a young man bound on a similar errand to call for me early in the morning, so I went to bed as soon as I had finished eating to get as much sleep and rest as possible. It was well that I did, for long before dawn creaking footsteps approached our tent and the man called out, 'Are you ready?' I quickly slipped on my leggings and moccasins, put on my robe, slung the pack over my shoulders, and we started.

"To avoid the drifts, we followed the ridges, but even there the snow lay deep, and we were continually breaking through the hard crust. My friend turned every mishap into a joke and broke the monotony of our travel with humorous tales and incidents. Late at night we camped in the bend of a small, wooded stream. We gathered a big pile of dry branches, kindled a roaring fire, and roasted some of the jerked meat. When supper was over, we dried our moccasins, then piling more wood on the fire, we wrapped ourselves up in our robes and went to sleep.

"I do not know how long we might have slept had we not been wakened by the howling of hundreds of wolves not far away from us. 'They're singing to the morning star!' said my friend. 'It is near day, so we must be up and going.'

"We ate a little of the pemmican, helped each other to load, and again we started. Before night we were overtaken by other men and boys who were also going to the relief of their friends in the other camp, where we arrived just in time to save many of the people from starving.

"How curious it was that the predictions of the holy man should come true — the stopping of the storm before morning, the forest, and the shadowy forms of animals. Stranger still was the death of the murderer. This took place, we were told by the people we had rescued, on the very night of the augury in our camp. They said, as the man was sitting in his tent that night, the wind suddenly blew the door flap violently aside, an expression of terror came over his face, he fell backward, and he was dead.

"In the old days, many strange things came to pass in the life of our people, but now we are getting to be different."

Wa-du-pa thanked the story teller, and we were about to go when Ne-ne-ba, pointing to Ja-bae-ka, whispered, "He's gone to sleep! Let's scare him."

The old man fell into the spirit of the fun, so we all tip-toed to the back part of the lodge where it was dark and watched as the flames died down to a blue flickering. We could see the boy's head drop lower and lower until his nose nearly touched his knee. Just then a log on the fire suddenly tumbled from its place, broke in two, sent up a shower of crackling sparks, and Ja-bae-ka awoke with a start. He threw up his head, looked all around, and thinking he was left alone in the darkened lodge, took fright and rushed to the door with a cry of terror. We ran out of our hiding places with shouts of laughter and overtook Ja-bae-ka outside the door, where we teased him about going to sleep and being afraid in the dark.

Suddenly he turned upon Ne-ne-ba and said, "You did that, you rascal! I'll pay you back sometime."

A Buffalo Ride

In this story, a grandfather relates a humorous episode of his youth, occasioned by a failed winter hunt by the Poncas. The narrator and his friend, who have lovers in the Ponca camp, anticipate a rendezvous — the common mode of courtship. Their "restless hearts" lead to their journey to meet the returning party and to the unexpected ride. La Flesche's diaries indicate that he worked on this story in early 1901 and sent it to the Youth's Companion, which did not publish it. Much of the language in the early passages is similar to that in the opening section of "The Laughing Bird." Also, this narrative follows the plot line of "The Story of a Vision," with significant modifications: courtship rather than concern for family causes the journey, Poncas rather than Omahas are hungry, and the story turns on humor. La Flesche made these changes to create a new story for his perceived audience in the Youth's Companion, and they offer an excellent opportunity to observe the writer's narrative skills.

ONE STORMY NIGHT WHEN Ja'-bae-ka, Ne-ne'-ba, and I were at A-di'-ta's lodge, he teased his grandfather to tell us a true story, something that happened when he was young.

The wind roared and shrieked outside, and we piled the wood high on the fire until the flames leaped and the sparks chased each other in a lively fashion through the opening at the top of the dome-shaped roof and our shadows danced merrily against the wall of the large, circular room. The old man blew the burnt tobacco out of his pipe, polished the bowl with the corner of his robe, and then we knew he was ready, so we all settled down to listen.

"It was at the time of the deep snow," he began, "long before any of you little ones were born. The Ponkas were hunting buffalo away out among the sand hills. A few families, under a foolish leader, left the tribe and went off to hunt by themselves. For a long time we heard nothing of them until one evening a man brought word that they had failed to find game and were now making for our camp.

"On hearing this news, I became restless. My heart kept going toward the other camp, drawn in that direction by a certain young woman that A-di´-ta's grandmother knows."

Here the old man's face brightened as he glanced at his wife, who turned her head to hide a smile.

"I went to the tent of Ke´-ma-ha, a friend of mine," continued the story teller, "and told him I was going to the other camp on a visit. The moment he heard my story he exclaimed, 'I'll go with you. Be ready at dawn.' He too had a restless heart.

"As soon as I returned to my tent, I went to bed, but sleep did not come easily, and I lay half conscious of all the sounds about me. Long before morning I heard the creak of approaching footsteps on the hard snow. I knew it was Ke´-ma-ha. I hurriedly arose, slipped on my moccasins and leggings, girded my robe about me, and met him at the door of the tent.

"With rapid strides we followed the well-beaten paths and, when we came to the end of these, made for the ridges to avoid the deep drifts. By the time the moon went down and the sun arose, the camp was far behind us. We traveled all day, turning every mishap into a joke, and at night we camped in a little grove by a small stream, built a roaring fire, cooked our supper, dried our moccasins, and went to bed.

"I was sound asleep when I was suddenly awakened by the howling of wolves all around us. 'That's the way they do when the big star [morning star, or Venus] comes up,' said my companion. 'It must be near day. Let's be going.'

"Once more we started upon our journey long before morning, and again we saw the moon go down and the dawn turn into day as we traveled on. Toward noon, as we were climbing a hill, my friend, who was ahead of me, suddenly dropped to the ground. I hastened to him and asked, 'What is it?'

" 'Buffalo!' he whispered, pointing beyond the hill.

"I peered over, and there between two deep ravines stood four bulls, motionless.

" 'Let's play a joke on them; they're sound asleep,' said Ke'-ma-ha, his eyes twinkling with mischief. 'We'll crawl up and charge upon them with a yell and make them flounder in the drift!'

"It was difficult to approach the huge creatures without making a noise, but they were dead asleep. So close did we steal up to them that we could see the frost of the night still on their backs and the smoke shooting out of their nostrils as they breathed. When we were near enough, we rushed forward, tossing our robes in the air and shouting at the top of our voices. The frightened animals plunged pell mell into the nearest ravine and tumbled madly about. We shouted with laughter between our yells at their wild attempts to climb over each other to solid ground. After a desperate struggle, three of the bulls scrambled up the bank, and away they went in that funny gallop of theirs, turning their heads from side to side, and their little tails flying in the air.

"Just for the fun of it, I ran to the remaining bull and sprang upon his back. I dug my heels between his ribs, buried my hands in his long hair, and held fast. He writhed, snorted and bellowed with rage, and made frantic efforts to strike me with his horns. Again and again he tried to shake me off, but I held on. All of a sudden he ceased struggling and lowered his huge body as though to lie down, but, with a mighty effort, he gave a tremendous leap, then another and another until he mounted the bank.

"What a fool I was not to let go then and tumble off! Instead of that, I clung all the tighter. The moment he touched hard ground, the bull sprang forward, and away he went like the wind, now and again kicking out viciously with his hind legs. How he did go! The earth seemed to spin like a top, and my hair whirled and whistled about my face so that I could scarcely see.

"A horrible thought rushed through my mind; what if the beast did not stop running until he dropped dead! He might run all day, and at night I would be far from human help. With no way to make a fire, I would freeze to death. My body would be found doubled up and stiff!

"A new danger arose before me with startling suddenness. I cried out in terror as I felt myself flying through the air. There was a confusion of horns, hoofs, and tails, a fearful thud; my head struck something, and it became dark.

"When I opened my eyes, they met those of my friend. 'Are

you alive? Are you hurt?' he cried, hastily passing his hands over my head, arms, and legs.

" 'I'm all right,' I answered, sitting up. 'Where's the bull?'

"Ke'-ma-ha burst out laughing as he said, 'I'm glad you're not hurt! He jumped down that high bank with you, and you went head first into the deep drift; that's the only thing that saved you. I saw the bull galloping away as I ran up. It's a wonder you're alive!'

"It was a wonder, for as I looked back, I saw that the bank was higher than a tall tree. The gods were not ready for me then, so I am here, telling you youngsters the story!"

A Buffalo Hunt

The preparations that attended the buffalo hunt form the backdrop for this story, which opens with a runner reporting to the "priest," or wathoⁿ′, *who was the director of the hunt and whose mark of office was his staff, a pole about eight feet long, crooked on the end and adorned with feathers and other objects. He chose the line of march, the campsites, and the runners who searched for and reported on the herds. When the runners returned, they reported to him confidentially so that he might have independent verifications of the location and size of the herd. The people were then notified of a surround, a process by which the herd was surrounded and the animals cut off as they attempted to escape. Officers were selected to maintain order. When the people drew near the herd, the officers' duty was to prevent camp noises that might frighten the herd and to keep individuals from slipping out of camp to hunt on their own. It was also their task to restrain the hunters until the signal for the charge on the herd was given.*

Hunters approached the herd in four stages, stopping each time for the wathoⁿ′ *and the chiefs to sit and ask* Wakoⁿ′da *for success. The pauses also had a practical side: to counteract the impatience exhibited by the narrator of the story and others. Besides checking excitement and precipitous action, they ensured a more successful hunt. The hunters were assisted by boys who tended the horses and helped in transporting the meat to camp.*

La Flesche apparently drew on his own childhood experiences for some details in this story. Among his papers in the Smithsonian Institution is an untitled four-page manuscript that appears to be an autobiographical statement recounting an episode much like the one described here.

"Ho, runner returning!" shouted a man, pointing toward the hills. The great cavalcade came to a standstill. "Let's go hear!" exclaimed little Wa'-du-pa, and we ran forward, jumping over tentpoles and dogs, until all out of breath we stood with the throng awaiting the runner.

On came the young man with sweeping strides; he approached the tribal priest, who stood leaning upon a staff, and whispered to him the report. The priest turned and in a low tone repeated it to the chiefs, who sat in front of the eager crowd. After a hurried consultation, the chiefs bade the herald proclaim that a herd had been found and a surround commanded. While the herald was calling the names of the officers appointed to keep order, Wa'-du-pa and I rushed back as fast as we could scamper.

"A surround is ordered!" we shouted as we ran to my father.

"Hurry!" he replied; "Bring in the gray and the black." It took but a moment to do so, and Wa'-du-pa's father and my uncle, who were to ride them, quickly mounted and galloped away.

Father made ready two slow and poky pack horses for us boys to ride to the men and bring home the hides and meat. As we moved forward, he called, "Don't go where you have no business. Stay with the other boys."

"All right!" we cried, bringing down our whips with a crack on the flanks of the old beasts; they made a pretense at a gallop but soon settled down to a hard, shake-up trot. Up and down the hills we went, laughing and chaffing, now and then catching glimpses of the Platte River shining in the sun.

Greatly to our disgust, the chiefs, followed by the hunters, made four pauses for religious observances on approaching the herd. After the fourth, we pushed on rapidly and were ascending a hill when a strong breeze struck us. Instantly, the hundreds of horses pricked up their ears, arched their necks, and became difficult to control.

"Hold back! Hold back! Steady there!" arose the stern voices of the officers, and their whips fell with resounding whacks upon the naked shoulders of some of the men at the front who had become disorderly; but the horses, mad with excitement, went faster and faster. As far as we could see there was a solid mass of men and horses. We were in the midst of it all, a place where Wa'-du-pa and I had no business to be. Our horses were no longer pokes, but like the best of those around us, they pranced with impatience.

All of a sudden a loud voice cried; "Na-wa! Na-wa!" Then, as though shot from a bow, every horse sprang forward, and away we went like the wind, making a noise as of rumbling thunder.

"Out of the way there, you little fools!" shouted someone behind us, but though we tugged and jerked at the reins, we could turn our horses neither to the right nor to the left. So thick was the cloud of dust that we could hardly see an arm's length. Suddenly, there was a terrific crash; we were upon the herd. The clatter of hoofs and horns, together with the loud panting of thousands of panic-stricken beasts, made a sound like the roaring of a tempest. Bang! Bang! went the guns; Ping! Zip! Whiz! flew the bullets and arrows around our heads. Wa'-du-pa cried out in terror.

I did not know whether we were going straight ahead, or round and round, up hill or down, but all at once our horses slackened speed, the roaring ceased, the cloud of dust floated upward, and — what a sight we saw! Pillowed upon one another lay the buffalo, here, there, and everywhere. "Oh! Look! Look!" I exclaimed. "I don't want to look; it's horrible!" cried Wa'-du-pa. With tail and mane flying in the air, a horse was galloping madly around, shying and snorting furiously at its own vitals which hung out of a great rent in its side. A man lay on the ground stunned, and a buffalo stood close by, bleeding from nostrils and mouth. The horse stumbled, fell, and became motionless; the buffalo, coughing violently, tottered forward and dropped dead.

"Wa'-du-pa, ho!" someone called.

"I'm coming!" shouted my companion, who whipped his horse and trotted away. Just at that moment I heard my uncle's voice, and I hurried to him. He had killed two fat cows and had already dressed the meat and hides for packing, so that as I rode up, he at once loaded the horses, and we were soon on our way toward camp.

At a shallow ravine we came upon a man on the edge of the bank while below stood a bull and a cow, both badly wounded. "What's the trouble? Why don't you kill the bull first and then the cow?" asked my uncle.

"I would if I had more arrows; I have only one left," replied the man. "The bull persistently keeps between me and the cow."

"Give me the bow and arrow," said my uncle. "Now, go around, as though to menace the cow."

The man did so, and the bull shifted his position, thus exposing her to the real danger. My uncle drew the bow, and with a hurtful thud the arrow pierced the side of the cow; there was a convulsive movement, a rattling cough, and the creature fell dead. The bull staggered to his mate, smelled of the body, licked the wound, then heaving a few gasps, he dropped to the ground lifeless. I turned to hide my tears at this pitiful sight.

Hundreds of fires were burning when we entered the camp at dusk. My mother had supper ready and bade me eat, but I insisted on waiting for Wa'-du-pa, who had not yet returned. At last, I heard his voice and called him to come and take supper with me, and he and I had a feast all to ourselves by the light of our own campfire.

"You stay here and sleep with me," I said, as he made a motion to go.

"All right!" he replied. We spread his blanket upon the ground, out in the open air, and covered ourselves with mine, using a bundle of grass for a pillow.

"Oh! There's a star; it's mine!" said Wa'-du-pa, stretching himself out.

"No, it isn't," I protested. "I saw it first."

"No, you didn't," he rejoined.

"Well, keep your old star. There comes the moon. That's mine!"

A Discovery and an Experience

Children were trained in an elaborate system of proper forms of kinship address, which made clear the relationships between individuals. Mistakes in usage were considered impolite. The deliberate breach of etiquette by the two boys in this story reflects the mischievousness to which they are prone as they lie idly about the lodge, counting rafters and playing the little game designed to strengthen the lungs. The mother knows that it is time for them to take up the more serious activity of learning to hunt. Thus she capitalizes on their mischievousness by chiding them indirectly and then pretending not to know their purpose as they retrieve corn from the cache just outside the lodge entrance in preparation for making wa'çke, *the pounded corn and honey mixture, to take on their excursion. Their lack of experience is reflected in not only their encounter with the hornets' nest but also their ignoring small game in their desire to kill the deer, which they lack the skill to hunt.*

Ke'-ma-ha lay with his cousin in the back part of the lodge on a rude couch covered with bear skins and buffalo robes. Being sons of two sisters, they should have addressed each other as brother according to the system of kinship among their people, and as etiquette required, but they called each other friend. The two idly amused themselves by counting the black rafters of the roof until they tired of that; then they took up a flat stick, the length of an arrow, having on one edge little notches from one end to the other. Ta-day'-ta, who happened first to take the stick, drew a long breath and then placing a fingernail on the first notch, moved it to the next and so on by regular intervals of time, repeating all the while in a monotonous tone the meaningless word *du-ah*, *duah*, *duah*, *du-ah* until he reached two-thirds of the length of the stick without once stopping to draw breath. Ke'-ma-ha then took the stick and repeated *duah* as his cousin did and reached the end without drawing breath.

The mother, who sat by the firelight sewing, arose to stir the jerked meat that was boiling in a kettle over the fire.

"We have not had any fresh meat for a long time, and I am hungry for some," said the woman as she took her seat and resumed her work. "In the early evening I saw two boys coming home with a raccoon and a turkey. If I had two smart boys, they too would go hunting and bring home raccoons, and I would have fresh meat."

The lads nudged each other as they heard this last remark. They now sat up and held a serious conversation in low tones. They had never been far away from home, and although they had heard of the hunting exploits of big boys and young men, they had never thought of going on a hunt. Their fathers, who had always provided fresh meat, were now away from home visiting another tribe and would not return for some time. The boys agreed to go hunting the next day, but did not let the mother know their determination.

"Come, brothers. Sit down and eat," called the woman to the lads as she had dished out the dried tripe, sweet corn, and broth from the kettle into wooden dishes. The cousins came to the fireside and ate out of a large wooden bowl between them. The firelight cast fantastic shadows against the sides of the house, and the sparks chased each other up to the opening at the top, as the three set to their simple evening meal.[1] When they had eaten, Ke'-ma-ha said, "Mother, can brother and I have some corn? We are hungry for parched corn."

"How can you be hungry? You have just had a meal," said the woman.

"But we want to make some wa-shan'-gae (pounded corn)," rejoined the lad, not knowing how else to keep his secret from his mother.

"There is no corn in the house, but you can find some in the cache," said the mother. "But be sure and fasten the entrance securely as you come out. I shall go out for a visit; do not go away, but take care of the house till I return."

The boys went to the cache, found the corn, broke half a dozen ears from a bunch, and returned to the house. The mother had gone, so they were alone. Each provided himself with a long, sharp stick, thrust it into the butt end of the cob, and set to work roasting the ears over the live coals. When every corn was richly browned, the boys shelled the corn and then pounded the kernels into meal. One went to the back part of the house and brought forth a wooden vessel filled with wild honey. This they poured into the meal and out of this mixture made a number of balls which they placed in a skin bag. Then they went to bed.

It was yet dark when Ta-day'-ta awoke. His cousin still lay breathing heavily in sleep. The lad lay awake for some time when he heard toward the outskirts of the village the sharp yelp and cry of a coyote, then almost immediately an answer to it in another direction. Then the dogs of the village took up the howl. This was the signal for the boys to rise, so Ta-day'-ta shook his cousin, saying in a smothered tone, "Wake up, wake up. The coyotes and the dogs have howled, the great star is up, and it is time for us to go." Ke'-ma-ha sat up and rubbed his eyes. Then remembering his plan for the day, he arose and took down his quiver, which hung up on a post; his cousin also took his quiver and the bag of corn balls, and the two started out on their hunt. Both were excited, for it was their first real adventure. They avoided the well-beaten paths for fear of attack by war-parties who might be lurking about.

When they had reached the bluffs overlooking the forest for which they were making, the dawn appeared, beautifying the sky with its rich color and promising fine weather for the day to follow. The boys sat down and ate a few of their corn balls, and then they entered the forest just as the sun arose. As they went into the woods, the boys strung their bows, then separated but kept within hearing distance of each other. Now and then they came upon the fresh tracks of deer, and as they were ambitious for large game, they followed the trails but could not find the animals. Once they scared up a flock of turkeys, but they wanted deer so paid little attention to the birds.

Ta-day'-ta was on a track which he was sure was made that very morning. The animal could not be far away; the sounds of a rabbit scurrying to cover or a squirrel scampering to a tree set his little heart to throbbing violently with expectancy. He would reach to his quiver for an arrow only to discover when he had strung it that he had been fooled by a "bad" little rabbit or squirrel. The tracks led him down to a ravine; they seemed to be fresher than ever. He strung an arrow to his bow so as to be ready to shoot should the deer start up or should he see it standing before him. There was caution in every step he took. When he had reached the bottom of the ravine, he stopped to peer into the tall weeds when something the like of which he had never seen or heard before attracted his attention. It was a thing new and strange to him. It hung suspended to the limb of a low-branching willow. The shape of it was like a large oval ball, twice the size of his head and the color a dull gray. The lad whistled, imitating the cry of a bird, a signal agreed upon by the young hunters. Ke'-ma-ha stealthily hurried to his cousin, who with an inquiring expression silently pointed to the strange object. Ke'-ma-ha looked puzzled, then shook his head. The boys stood watching the queer and innocent-looking thing as it swayed to and fro in the breezes that stirred the leaves of the tree upon which it hung. "Shoot it," whispered Ke'-ma-ha to his cousin.

Ta-day'-ta put an arrow to his bow and drew the string almost up to his ear when his cousin put his hand out to him and exclaimed in an undertone, "Hold on, hold on, don't shoot! It might prove to be dangerous, and we might not be able to get back the arrow if you should hit it. Wait now and I will hit it with a stone." So saying, he took from his belt a sling and out of a leather bag a pebble; this he put into the sling, which he now swung round and round with his right arm. Then, with all his might he released the stone at the curious object. "Whiz-z-z-z, chuck!" and the stone plunged into the thing, leaving a dark and jagged hole behind it. The boys awaited results. They had not long to wait. A tiny black speck with yellow streaks came out of the hole, turned once, twice, then there was a flash, and — zip! Something struck Ke´-ma-ha on the eyebrow. Instantly he felt as though his head would burst with pain, and he fell to the ground and rolled about, howling all the while. In the meantime another black speck streaked with yellow had appeared on the surface of the ball. It too skirmished around for a second, with a flash it disappeared, and zip! It struck Ta-day´-ta on his bare breast, and he too fell to the ground and mingled his cries with that of his cousin. The boys covered their little heads with their robes. They peeped out and saw that the gray ball was now covered with the little black and yellow things, and flashes were darting out from their midst.

"Let's run," said Ta-day´-ta to his cousin, and immediately they arose and ran away as fast as they could go, covering their heads as they went.

When their throbbing pains had subsided and their tears dried, the lads again followed deer tracks; one led them to a clump of bushes. They cautiously approached it, but they had not thought to do so from the lee side. As they drew near, there was a rustle of leaves, then a crash. The boys rushed forward, but the buck they had scared up was already far beyond the reach of arrow.

NOTE

1. The language of much of this sentence appears also in "The Laughing Bird" and "A Buffalo Ride."

Kae-zhin-ga: A Story of the Platte River

Children were carefully disciplined and could expect punishment for breaches of discipline, including such acts as taking items that belonged to their elders without permission or besieging one with a barrage of questions, as the boy does in this story. However, it is something in the concentration on his whittling and his pert attitude that reminds the Yankton scout of his own son at home and, ultimately, saves the family. An earlier version of this story, titled "The Red Arrow," is among La Flesche's literary manuscripts in the Smithsonian Institution.

UNTIL THE BEGINNING OF THE LAST century very little was known to the English-speaking people of the country west of the Missouri. It was generally thought of as a barren wilderness, void of any human interests. It is true there were no cities with roads leading to them from different directions, there were no farms such as we see nowadays wherever we go, and the railroad was not dreamed of yet. Every stream or prominent butte had a name which recorded some event of tragedy or happy delivery from danger. Along the Platte and the Loup the Pawnees had their villages; along the Missouri, the Elkhorn, and the Niobrara, the Omaha had theirs; while to the northward dwelt the Sioux. The people who made their homes on these streams had no printed literature, but the land itself was their book upon which was written the story of each tribe, full of human pathos.

It was at a time when the western country was "wild," and there were no white people except a few traders, but there were buffalo, elk, deer, and wolves and — Indians. And it was at a time of the year when the trees had dropped their leaves, and the grasses on the hills had turned brown, and the rivers were covered with ice. Well hidden among the willows and cottonwood trees that grew thick along the banks of the "Wide Water," or Platte River, stood a solitary teepee, yellowed with the smoke of many fires. Within this smoke-stained dwelling sat a little, wee bit of a boy all alone, whittling a stick with his mother's big knife and littering the fire-place with the shavings. The chastisements he received for playing with sharp-edged and pointed tools were frequent, but his fascination for his mother's knife and awl was stronger than his fear of punishment, so his disobedience was persistent when the desire for whittling and punching came upon him. To his father and mother and other near relatives he was "little brother" and so called by them, but to strangers and persons not his kin he answered to the name Kae-zhin-ga, which, put into English, would mean Little Turtle.

Now and then Little Turtle whistled a tune of his own making as he worked, for the thought of the slapping he was sure to get when his mother came home was far from his wayward little mind. Nothing disturbed his guilty happiness, not even the sleep-enticing tattoo played by the morning breeze with the smoke-flaps of the teepee.

All of a sudden the frame of the door-flap fell with a dull thud, and a man entered and seated himself near the fire just as Kae-zhin-ga pressed with all his might the sharp edge of the knife against the stick he was cutting. Crack! it went, and the severed part flew away and struck the visitor right on the chest.

"I didn't mean to do that," said the boy in apology. "It went so quick I couldn't stop it."

The stranger muttered something which the boy did not understand. Then, after a moment's pause, the lad spoke again. "You see those?" pointing at a row of rawhide packs lying along the back part of the teepee. "They are full of dried deer meat, beaver meat, and all kinds of skins."

The man gave a nod and a sort of grunt, and Kae-zhin-ga went on.

"My father is a hunter and a trapper. Early in the morning, before the big star comes up, he goes to set his traps, and then he goes to hunt for deer. He is out now. He's out all the time, even when the wind blows hard and the snow whirls around like ghosts. Did you ever see beavers? They live in little houses along the banks of the river. They cut down big trees with their teeth, then they cut the branches in short pieces and pile them up in the water across the streams so they could eat the bark in the winter when it is cold and they are hungry. The little beavers have their own paths to the eating places, and the big ones have theirs. A good trapper ought to know this because then he would catch the big ones instead of the little ones. I know all about the ways of the beavers. Sometimes when my father is at home in the evenings and my mother is drying his moccasins by the fire and he is smoking his pipe, he tells my big brother all about the beavers and their ways. They think I'm asleep when they are talking, but I lie awake and listen. That's how I know. When I get big, I'm going to be a trapper like my father. Where did you come from?"

There was no answer, but the boy, intent upon his whittling, kept on with his chatter. "You needn't tell me if you don't want to. When my father is out hunting and trapping, my mother takes her hoe and goes into the woods to get wild beans. There's a kind of mice that gathers lots of beans and put them away in little houses under the ground because when the snow comes and the ground is frozen they would have something to eat till the summer comes again. This is the way my mother finds the little houses. She looks on the ground under the tall grass and sees a tiny ridge. Under it is the path of the mice. She follows the little ridge till she comes to a small hump in the ground. She thrusts a sharp stick into it, and if it feels soft inside, she will not break it open because it's the nest where the mice live. Then she follows the ridge the other way and comes to another hump, and that's where the beans are. She breaks open the house at the back side and takes half of the beans and covers up the hole again, and that's the way she gets beans for us. When my father and mother are away, I stay at home to take care of the teepee so it won't burn up. It's awful to have your things and teepee burn up. Why don't you say something? Don't you ever talk?"

The little fellow looked up and saw that his visitor had gone, and in the spot where he had sat there stood something that made him open his eyes wide with wonder. It was an arrow stuck in the ground and standing upright. The shaft up to the feathers was smeared with red paint like dripping blood. The youngster rushed out with the knife still in his hand, and there near the door stood his father and mother, just about to throw down their burdens. "What is it, little brother?" asked the father.

"There's been a man here," replied Kae-zhin-ga breathlessly, "and talked to me for the longest time. His face was painted red. I saw him when he first came in, then I went on cutting my stick and when he heard you coming, he turned himself into an arrow, and there he stands by the fire."

"You have been dreaming," said the father, bending low to enter the teepee, but true enough, there stood the arrow by the fireside. The man snatched it up, examined it closely, and quickly recognized it as a Sioux arrow. His face turned pale, for his people were then at war with the Sioux. A war party was near, and for some reason the scouts had, in this manner, given him warning to flee.

"Quick," he said to his wife. "Pull down the teepee and get the saddle ready. I will go after the horses!"

For a moment the woman pressed the child closely to her bosom with the fervor of a mother's love and then set to work pulling the teepee down, folding the cover into a square pack, and tying the poles together.

She had hardly finished when the trapper ran in with the horses. They were hastily saddled and packed, and soon the father, the mother, and the little son were in full flight, not down the river by which they had come, but across the prairies, far away from the paths usually traveled by hunters. The shadow of evening came upon them, then the darkness of night, and yet they traveled on and on toward the Omaha country, toward their home.

Far down the river, which Kae-zhin-ga's father and mother in their flight avoided as dangerous, in a woody bend lay the camp of the Pawnees in unsuspecting slumber. As the morning star rose above the horizon, the sharp cry of a coyote broke the stillness of the night. It was followed by the moanlike howl of a gray wolf; then all the dogs of the camp replied, filling the hills with dismal echoes. Gradually this doleful chorus diminished to an occasional bark or whine, and then the night fell again into silence, save for the sighing of the wind among the leafless trees.

Suddenly, the hills vibrated with a shout, clear and prolonged; it was the signal for attack. A hundred voices answered with the war cry; then there was a rush of many feet.

The camp was instantly thrown into noisy confusion. Women, grasping their little ones, fled hither and thither while the warriors seized their weapons and ran to meet the foe. The crashing of war clubs against bullhide shields, the whizzing of arrows, the cries of terror and of pain, and the shouts of triumph filled the air until the eastern sky was red with the dawn.

The sun arose and touched the upturned faces of the dead with its soft rays. A wounded warrior, bending low, clutched the frosty grass with both hands. His body swayed from side to side, his head, crested with the feathers of the owl, drooped lower and lower, his face touched the earth, and he lay motionless in death. As though by magic the sky above became alive with birds. The crows, flying on a level with the tops of the hills, called noisily to each other. Higher up the buzzards and the eagles soared in wide, sweeping circles waiting till they could safely descend to enjoy the feast provided by the thunder [war] gods.

It was the harvest time of the year. The brown hills were veiled in a bluish haze, and from the tops of the mound-shaped earth lodges of the Omaha village smoke curled lazily upward and mingled with the blue above. On scaffolds of poles, near the entrance of each dwelling, hung great bunches of red, blue, and white ears of corn drying in the sun and wind. Through the intervening spaces between the lodges children chased each other and played hide-and-seek, the brown skins and black hair glinting in the sunlight. Along the outskirts of the village young men played at hoop and javelin,[1] shouting in triumph at a point made or noisily disputing a doubtful one.

Following each other in single file ten men entered one of the largest lodges. They were visitors from the Yankton, a tribe that dwelt in a far-off country. The host greeted each one and motioned him to a seat by the fire in the center of the wide circular room. A pipe was filled and lighted and passed around while the strangers recounted with zest the humorous incidents of their journey.

"Were any of you in the battle on the Wide Water fought between your tribe and the Pawnee not quite a year ago?" asked the host when there was a pause in the talk. "I want to hear about it."

All the eyes of the visitors turned to a little man with a hooked nose, and one quietly said, "There is the man who can tell you all about it. He was in that fight."

"Hae, coda!" (Ah, friend!) said the small man after a moment's reflection, "I hesitate, for shame, to speak of that battle, for my part in it turned out to be very much like that of a woman, but I will tell you what I know about it.

"We had quite worn out our moccasins when we reached the Pawnee country; we had travelled hard and far. When we entered the land of our enemy, the younger men were no longer sent as scouts; men who had been many times on the war-path were chosen. One night as I lay sound asleep, I was suddenly brought to my feet by two men. They took me to the leader, who sat by a low fire. He at once offered me the sacred pipe of war, and as I put the stem to my lips, he repeated to me the solemn words that bound a scout to report truthfully all he should see or that should happen to him while on duty. I took four good whiffs to signify my assent and appealed to the gods of war who dwell at the four corners of the earth. Two other men had already gone through the ceremony and were waiting for me. The leader gave to each his route, and we three started out in the darkness. I was told to take the river.

"I travelled swiftly, keeping close to the edge of the water, and soon I left the camp far behind me. Just about day-break I was startled by cracking sounds and heavy breathing. I peered cautiously over the edge of the bank, and there within only a few paces stood a man piercing the ice with a heavy spear. He soon made a good-sized hole and thrust his bare arm into the cold water to set a trap. I could have killed him and counted the act as a deed of valor, but it would have been contrary to my orders. So I left the man and hastened to find his camp and see if there were others with him or horses worth capturing. I found a small herd, which I hastily counted, and then hurried on to find the camp and came upon a single teepee in the woods under a sheltering bluff, which showed that there was but one family. I stole softly to the door and peeped in and saw only a little boy sitting all alone by the fire whistling and whittling a stick. He gave me just a glance as I entered and went on with his cutting and spoke to me without raising his eyes. His round cheeks, the cut of his hair, his manner of whittling and whistling were [so] very like my own little O-he-de-ga that all the stern thoughts of war, of killing, burning, capturing of horses fled from me and left my heart as tender as that of a woman. It seemed as though I was in my own teepee with my own little boy and bound to protect him. The little fellow won my heart, and I yielded to the temptation to violate my promise to tell my leader all that happened. I determined, regardless of consequences, not to let the boy or his people be killed by our warriors. Drawing from my quiver an arrow, I hastily stained it red and thrust it in the ground near the fire as a warning to the father. When I left, the little one was still talking, never raising his eyes.

"The sun had reached the middle of heaven when I met our war party. I went straight to the leader to make my report. 'Hae, coda! who can deceive the thunder gods who control the wars and battles and know even the innermost thoughts of men!'

" 'Speak the truth,' said the leader as I stood before him, 'and walk the earth without fear. Speak falsely and death shall soon overtake you or yours with violence.'

"I made my report with all the warriors standing around me and told of the things that I saw and did, even to the minutest detail, save the warning I gave the people of the lonely teepee. I finished. I wandered not from the truth as far as I went.

" 'Is that all?' asked the leader gravely.

"The question awakened in me a sense of guilt and fear, but I answered boldly, 'That is all I can tell.'

" 'Hy, hy, hy!' said the leader, solemnly raising his spread hands to the sky and as solemnly lowering them to the earth in sign of gratitude to those mystic powers for his good fortune.

"A scout was sent to watch the people I had found, and we moved on, but my heart was filled with fear lest the father of the little boy should not understand the warning I had left him. The sun was fast falling upon the western hills when we saw in the distance the scout returning. He gave the signal that the people had fled, and I secretly rejoiced but a new fear arose in my mind when I remembered the warning of the leader against making a false report. When the leader heard from the scout that the people had fled, a frown of disappointment spread over his face as he said, 'We have lost a good chance, but we will move on to the village of the Pawnees, where we may have better luck.'

"The sun went down, it was dark, but we pushed on. About the middle of the night the warriors suddenly stopped. There were whisperings that the other two scouts had returned with the news that they had found the Pawnee camp and we were close upon it. Hurriedly, we strung our bows and tested them, then moved rapidly on with caution, and when the morning star arose, we rushed upon the camp.

"Ah, friend! They, too, were men; they had slept with their weapons and at the attack did not forget them. The women fled into the woods but the men stood by their teepees and fought courageously. We killed many, but our loss was as great as theirs. At the very first an arrow went through my body. I fell bleeding and unconscious.

"The fight, I was told, went on till the sun arose. The dead and dying lay scattered and dark upon the frosty ground. Most of our warriors won honors or captured booty. I was among the few who failed. All the way home I suffered agonies from my wound and became a burden to those who carried me away. It was a part of my punishment for withholding the truth from my war leader. But that was not all, for when we got home and I entered my teepee, I found my wife stricken with grief. My little boy, O-he-de-ga, lay dead."

The pipe came around to the warrior, and he smoked in silence.

The host arose, went to the post where his quiver was hanging, drew from it a red-stained arrow, and without a word handed it to the little man.

"Hae!" exclaimed the warrior, "this is my arrow, the very one I used to give warning to those people to flee. You are the man I saw that morning setting a trap. You did not know that danger was so near. And where is the little boy who did not get scared at the painted warrior?"

The arrow was passed around among the visitors, and while they were exclaiming over it, the host said, "Come here, little brother!" and Kae-zhin-ga, who as usual, was whittling a stick, trotted out from the shadowy part of the lodge and stood before his father.

The warrior grasped the child by the hand and said, "My little boy is gone, but I am glad that you are alive." There was a slight twitching of the lips and chin of the man as he released the little hand.

When the strangers had gone, the host sat smoking his long-stemmed pipe in contemplative silence while the black kettle that hung over the fire cheerily hummed and sputtered and breathed out savory odors. From the back part of the lodge came a woman's voice, "Little brother, where is my awl?" and Kae-zhin-ga stood puzzled, for he did not quite understand why the tone of impatience that usually came with those oft repeated words had changed so suddenly to one of motherly tenderness.

NOTE

1. This game, in which a javelin was thrown at a rolling hoop, was adopted from the Pawnees. See Fletcher and La Flesche, *The Omaha Tribe*, 366.

Tae-hon'-zhon

As setting for his story of Tae-hon'-zhon, La Flesche describes ritual
and physical training that were a part of the preparation for becoming
a warrior, including the obligatory non'zhinzhon rite, which every
male went through at puberty. It was an appeal to Wakon'da for help
throughout life. During four days of solitary fasting, the youth sang

Wakon'da thethu wahpathin atonhe
Wakon'da thethu wahpathin atonhe

which La Flesche translated as "Wakon'da, here in need I stand." The
vision that came to him might have been related to inanimate as well
as animate nature, and the phenomenon or creature held special
significance, such as the hawk, which was associated with success in
war as in the narrative below.

Preparations for going on the warpath were elaborate and for the
most part secretive. War parties were organized under the nu'don-
honga, or war leader, who assigned men to four classes of service,
including the moccasin carriers as in the story below. They were chosen
because of strength, which was required for the important task of
carrying the large amount of footwear necessary on long journeys.
Though most warfare was organized under a leader, a man might go
alone under special circumstances of sorrow following the death of a
close relative. One who was not part of an organized war party might
follow it and attempt to join, as Tae-hon'-zhon does below; his acceptance or rejection was left to the leader. Warriors could earn six grades
of war honors, including striking an unwounded or wounded enemy
with the hand or bow, striking a dead enemy with the hand or bow,
killing the enemy, taking his scalp, and beheading the corpse.

The story of Tae-hon'-zhon's first experience on the warpath is
based loosely upon the traditional "History of Icibaji," a version of
which Joseph La Flesche dictated to Dorsey. Like the traditional
warrior his first time at war, Tah-hon'-zhon joins the war party on

the trail, becomes a moccasin carrier, and kills a lone enemy with his
club; both earn reputations as warriors who strike fear into the hearts
of children.

ROM TIME IMMEMORIAL, THE ambition and aspirations of an
Indian boy was to become a great hunter, a warrior, or a
chief. The first step toward the attainment of one or all of
these distinctions was to seek for a sign of approval of the
life to be pursued from the Deity. This was done by seclusion
and fasting. As soon as a boy could clearly remember and give an
accurate account of events that took place for three or four years
back, he was ready for this trying ordeal. If he had parents, they
urged him to take the fast so that he might know that he will have
the aid of the Deity in all his enterprises through life. The father
even takes him to the place of seclusion and shows him how to
put the moistened clay upon his face and head, which is the sign
of humility, a condition of mind necessary in appearing before
the Great Invisible Power that moves and abides in all things. If
the boy is an orphan, he of his own volition takes upon himself
this suffering and search for a recognition from the Deity. Four
days is the longest duration of the fast. Night and day the
supplicant weeps and sings a song of prayer that was handed
down from countless numbers of generations. The answer to his
prayer comes in the form of a vision or a dream of some animal
or bird possessing powers not bestowed upon man. The dream
or vision of a hawk, eagle, or swallow is a sign that the supplicant
will have the approval and aid of the Deity in his warlike enterprises; if of a wolf or bear, he in battles will have the courage of

the animals, or if wounded, their vitality will strengthen him to recover from the wounds. These dreams or visions are to be remembered and brought into the spirit of the possessor of them only in the most pressing and distressing moments, when human courage and strength are on the point of failure.

The next step, and last, is the training of the physical forces of the body to the greatest endurance. This may be done either by exercises taken individually or by uniting with the society of young men who call upon each member to perform some difficult task, calculated to overcome some weakness known to be in the youth called upon to perform such task. To give strength to the hands and arms and to develop the lifting power, they had a game in which a heavy rock was swung between the legs and then thrown backwards over the head. Short-distance races for swift running and long-distance ones for endurance were often run, these latter sometimes lasting as long as half or a whole day. Swimming came almost naturally to the boys, but diving was often practiced. Carrying heavy weights at long distances was practiced. A man carrying a whole elk or half of a buffalo was considered a powerful man. It was necessary for the hunter to have the strength to carry the game that he kills. Frequently, he has had to carry the carcass of the animal he killed for many hours. There were numerous ways of developing the muscles, and young men organized societies in which all the games of running and lifting were practiced. The practice with the bow and arrow was almost a daily habit for the young men, and many of them became noted for their skill in the use of the bow.

Tae-hon'-zhon had had his vision, although he did not go

through the rite of seclusion and fasting. It happened in this way; he had a father who was unkind to him. In traveling, more weight was given him to carry than he could endure, so he had to rest frequently. He had a bird-hawk with a broken wing. When he sat down to rest, he busied himself with dressing the wound of the bird. The father became impatient at having to wait and call the boy so often.

When the boy came up one day, perspiring under his heavy burden and clinging to his captive bird, the father angrily stuck him and, snatching the bird from his hands, threw it in the air. The bird circled in the air for a moment and then flew beyond a hill. The boy, forgetting the painful blow with tears in his eyes, stood watching the flight of the bird until it disappeared. When camp was pitched, the boy stole out of the tent and went back to find his bird. He followed the trail of the returning hunters until he came to the spot where he was so cruelly punished; then it grew dark. Fearing that someone would be coming to find him, Tae-hon'-zhon hid himself in a bunch of tall grass, then went to sleep. During the night the boy heard strange noises and the thud of the hoofs of wild animals, but he covered his head with his little buffalo robe and imagined himself securely hid.

Early in the morning he followed the direction in which the little hawk went and came to the place where it disappeared. Thinking that it had dropped just beyond the brink of the hill, the lad went hunting through the grass. He heard a swish overhead as of fluttering wings, and he looked up and saw a bird-hawk swooping down upon a bird much larger than itself. The bird attacked flew low to the ground, and just as it passed the boy about an arm's length, the hawk gave it a resounding blow on the head with his beak, killing it instantly, and then flew on, giving the cry peculiar to its kind. Then it turned and came fluttering, finally lighting on the lad's shoulder. It was his little hawk; he recognized it, he reached out his hand tenderly to take it, but instantly the bird was on its wings and taking flight in the air. The boy sat watching it. On and on went the bird and smaller and smaller grew its size until in the distance it became a mere speck, and finally it vanished in the blue sky far beyond the hills. Being a thoughtful and serious-minded boy, Tae-hon'-zhon sat thinking of the incident, never withdrawing his eyes from the place where the form of the bird disappeared. Suddenly in his head came the thought and words "It is a vision, an incident that has a meaning deeper than an ordinary occurrence. It shall be to me that mystery which shall lead me out of this misery to the life of a warrior. My bird has left me, but it has also left in me an inspiration to become as fierce as he when he killed that bird dead at my feet. This I shall remember when I attack my enemies in battle and from the memory of it take courage."

Tae-hon'-zhon grew up to be a young man. All alone he would take exercises, short- and long-distance running, lifting, and he practiced daily with his bow and arrows. He always carried with him a heavy war-club, which had never been used, the only thing left him by his father when he died. At funeral races he took a number of prizes. He was called upon a number of times as a runner when the tribe was on its annual buffalo hunt.

Tae-hon'-zhon learned that a war-party had started out

against the Pa-dun-kas [Comanches]. The party had been gone three days, yet the young man started to overtake it and to apply to the leader for a place as moccasin-carrier. He traveled night and day, and after considerable difficulty, losing the trail and getting lost, he overtook the party. A scout reported that a young man had arrived. On ascertaining who the applicant for a place in the party was, the leader said, "Bring him into camp and give him a place; he will break the monotony of the march by amusing us." So the youthful warrior was given the humblest place in the camp. On the march, like other carriers, he had to carry the extra articles of clothing of the more experienced warriors, who were relieved of as much burden as was possible. This being the first experience of the young man in a war-party, he was often imposed upon and made to do ridiculous things outside of his legitimate business, just to create amusement for the warriors. This the young man could not resent because they were mixed up with the duties of camp. However, he remembered the abuses and toiled on like the rest. One thing they did was to compel the young man to carry the lieutenants across a stream on his back. This, however, was done without the knowledge of the leader, and he did not share in the mischief.

Early one morning the scouts reported that a solitary man was discovered. From his dress and the cut of his hair, he was recognized as a Pawnee warrior, evidently a scout of a war-party. That tribe being enemy to that to which the hero of this story belonged, preparations were made to kill the man. He was moving along a level country, so there was no way to get close enough to him to attack him without risk of his escaping. Tae-

hon'-zhon begged the leader to let him go and see the killing,
but was with impatience ordered to remain in his place with the
carriers of moccasins. But he followed the warriors at a distance
without their knowing it, carrying only the legacy left him by his
unkind father, the heavy war-club. When they came to the place
designated for the point of attack, the warriors stopped to lay
aside all impediments, and while thus engaged, Tae-hon'-zhon
with his war-club came up. The leader looked at him with a
frown, but the youthful warrior, being ready for the attack,
leaped forward, and with the swiftness of a hawk he was making
for the Pawnee. The warriors stood transfixed to the ground in
their amazement of the boldness of the youth and his sudden
attack.

The quick ear of the Pawnee caught the sound of snapping
grass and turned to behold his assailant coming upon him with
the swiftness of a bird. His first impulse was to run, and he did so,
but as he saw that there was only one man charging upon him,
and he with only a war-club, he turned to face his assailant. The
Pawnee had his bow strung; he reached back to draw an arrow
from his quiver, but instead of grasping an arrow he caught hold
of the end of the frame of the quiver and kept tugging at that.
The young warrior came with uplifted club, and as there was no
time to draw an arrow now, the Pawnee used his bow to ward the
blow. With a single stroke the bow was broken in two, and at the
next the war-club went crashing into the brains of the lonely
warrior, and he lay lifeless on the ground. It took but a moment
to remove his scalp, and not until then did the warriors recover
from their surprise, and they came running up. Then Tae-hon'-

zhon would not let them touch the body; he took all the honors himself. The youth lifted his war-club in a threatening attitude as one of the lieutenants came up, and he exclaimed, "I feel tempted to knock you to the ground as I have done this warrior. You may learn now that even a shy moccasin-carrier might become as combative as a grizzly."

So Tae-hon'-zhon was the only warrior of this party who returned to the village with war honors. After this he went on the war-path sometimes individually and sometimes as leader of a party and never returned without trophies. His adventures were many, and soon he became noted for his prowess among all the northwestern tribes. His name was mentioned with fear in all the tribes. Mothers quieted their children by simply mentioning his name. One dark and stormy night he was walking along the camp of his enemies, and just as he was passing a large tent, a fretting child was thrust out of the door by a woman with the words "Catch him, Tae-hon'-zhon, and carry him away." He did and carried the boy home. Tae-hon'-zhon gave his captive to a couple that were childless, and they adopted the child.

Tae-hon'-zhon was now an old man. He would sit at his fireside in the long winter evenings, and tell of his wonderful adventures to the youth of the village, who gathered around him and never tired of the exciting tales. Of narrow escapes he had many. His body was covered with scars, cuts from battle axes, wounds from arrows, and stabs from knives. His gestures, his facial expressions, and the language he used in his narratives added a warmth and zest to his stories that he never failed to thrill the hearts of his hearers, old and young. The aged warrior had two sons, one about seventeen and the other sixteen. All winter long he told his sons the story of his life, beginning with his vision of the hawk. He watched with interest the manner of the two boys as he related to them the battles in which he took part and of the honors he won in each. The older boy would soon grow restless and amuse himself in childish ways, but the younger boy would rivet his eyes upon the furrowed face of the chief and unconsciously move to get as near his father as possible so as not to lose a single word. The old warrior saw that there was in the youth the quality which was in every brave man. He was proud of the boy as he saw his possibilities although he had hoped that the older and handsomer of the two would turn out to be the man he desired to take his place as chief of the tribe.

It was one day in the summer noised about the camp that the Pa-dun-kas' camp was not far away, and that Gray-eagle, Tae-hon'-zhon's captive who had now grown up and become a famous warrior, had organized an army to go and fight them. The army was to start in the morning. Tae-hon'-zhon woke his boys and, throwing their quivers over their shoulders, said to them, "Our men are going to fight our enemies the Pa-dun-kas, led by the brave warrior, the Gray-eagle, whom you both know, and I want you to go and see the battle. Brave deeds will be done, and I wish you to see the leader, get as close to him as you can, as I wish you both to be like him. He is the man to watch and to take for an example. Now, my sons, come with me, and I will take you to him and ask that he permit you to join his army." So taking the youths by the hands, he took them to the tent of the great warrior.

There the army had gathered. Gray-eagle stood near his tent, talking to his men, and, as he saw Tae-hon'-zhon coming toward him with his two bright boys, he paused in his speech to receive the trio. The aged warrior addressed the younger and said, "Seeing you here and hearing you speak words of encouragement to your men revives the war-spirit in me, but not the sinews of my body, nor the sight of my eyes that now grow dim. Were I younger, the leadership would be mine, but unwillingly I yield to age that reduces even the bravest to a helpless creature. Here are two young men; I give them to you to join you in this great enterprise. I wish them to become like you and their old father. They are men, and it is the fate of men to face death at every turn. I do not ask you to look after them and to see that they return safe; I only ask that you permit them to see you in the battle to come; that is all I ask. I leave the rest to that Invisible Power that controls all men and beasts and even the thunder and lightning that sweep the earth with destruction. If it pleases him, as I hope it may, to see you return victorious, then shall these young men be honored, and I shall go to the spirit-land with a light heart and renewed youth. In all this great movement of life, I know that even the rock, in time, crumbles and disappears, the great tree falls to the earth and soon turns to dust in decay. There is an end to all things, the sun, moon, and stars, and the earth alone survives. So we, like other things, must yield, but with brave hearts, to the inevitable."

The old one then embraced his sons and turned to go but was addressed by the Gray-eagle, "You have yourself been a warrior and know the responsibilities of leadership in war; that in case of defeat, it is the place of the leader to give his life for the many. Those scars which I now see upon your body confirm this statement. I am willing that your sons should see me in battle, and I am touched by your confidence in me, but in case of defeat and they should lie with me, then I ask that your spirit reproach me not. The death of a warrior is the only death to be desired by men; it is a glorious one. Still, the heart of the father, even though he be a warrior, is often tender toward his youthful sons, and when by chance death overtakes one, some blame may be attached to someone; from this I ask you to release me, as a desire to please a noted warrior makes me to accept your offer."

The veteran simply said, "They go to do what their father should have done, so no blame shall attach to anyone."

Wa-ha-ton-ga

*Soon after a war party returned, those eligible for war honors partici-
pated in the* wate'giçtu *ceremony, which was presided over by the
keepers of the Packs Sacred to War. The warriors stood before the
packs, and the keepers reminded them to speak truthfully, lest their
time on earth be cut short. Each warrior recounted his acts in war
while holding a stick high over the sacred pack. At the end of his
recitation, he dropped the stick. If it fell on the pack and remained, the
pack had accepted his words as true. If it fell to the ground, the pack
had rejected the warrior's words and he was derided by the people.
Those earning war honors qualified to participate in the Warrior,
or* Hethu'shka, *dance society. In the dance, the men were adorned
with prescribed insignia that indicated the grade of honor they had
achieved. Sons of chiefs could represent their fathers at meetings of the
society, as apparently had Francis La Flesche, who supplied the ethnologist J. Owen Dorsey with several* Hethu'shka *songs and helped
him revise the translation of others. Though war was a serious affair,
the following story takes a humorous turn. The central figure is
addicted to the game of hoop and javelin, on which he gambles
excessively. He would rather spend his time in competing at thrusting
a stick through a rolling hoop and capturing it than engage in the
affairs of men. Ironically, however, he earns a high grade of war
honor in spite of himself.*

THE CAMP FIRES TWINKLED MERRILY in the dusk as though
vying with the stars that blinked at each other in the cloudless sky, and the murmur of many voices filled the air of the
quiet summer evening.

Around a blazing fire in front of Wa-ha-ton-ga's teepee had
gathered a number of men, old and young, to hear the oft-told

tales of the aged man, tales of battles, of marvelous escapes, and of hardships, tales that never failed to win the admiration or sympathy of men and to inspire the growing warriors with thoughts of brave deeds and acts of heroism.

Near the door of the teepee stood a pole upon which hung an old bull-hide shield that rattled in the occasional breezes. After some moments of silent reflection the furrowed face of the aged warrior brightened with an animated expression, and he began.

"We all know that when one has attained the years of manhood, he usually throws away his infant name and takes one that he has won by some act of bravery or generosity. If he so forgets his manly pride as to show cowardice in times of danger, the people change his name for him in contempt or derision. Listen now to the story of the changing of my own name and let the younger men judge whether I have fairly won my present name or not.

"No man was ever kinder to his children than my father was to me. Often times my conduct was such as would provoke any ordinary man to anger and severity, but never once did he speak a harsh word to me or hold over me a threatening hand. As for my mother, she was so tender hearted that she would weep at the sight of a bare-footed boy and give to him my leggings or moccasins, things that she had made with her own hands. I had all that a child could desire; all my wishes and foolish fancies were gratified by my fond parents. I passed the age of childhood and became a young man. The notches on the edge of my father's whip-handle, the record of my age, numbered seventeen, each notch representing one winter. In stature I was a man, but all my actions were yet those of a boy. Young men of my age were useful and active in helping their parents to secure food supplies and skins for clothing. But I was of no use to my parents or anybody else, and our neighbors spoke openly of their contempt for me.

About this time I became fascinated with a game, the hoop and javelin. I see young men playing it now. I gave all my time and thought to it. From morning till sundown I played it, and at night I dreamed hoop and javelin. My thighs and arms became as hard as the trunk of a tree from constant running and throwing. My father gave me a horse which he himself had broken. He expected me to ride it when the camp was on the march, but I chose to ride a slow-going old pony, for the young horse by its restlessness would interfere with the hoop and javelin game. My father and mother saw very little of me and instead of being a help and comfort to them, I caused them no end of anxiety and annoyance. Not satisfied with playing the game simply for amusement, I fell to playing for stakes, and I usually lost. The men to whom I lost went to my father and mother to collect their winnings, and without a murmur the moccasins, leggings, or arrows were turned over to them. At one time I lost a fine pack-horse at the game. Even then my father spoke not a word of reproach or protest. Hunger drove me to my home late one afternoon, having gone to the game without my morning meal. My father had just finished a lance trimmed with otter skin and eagle feathers and was at work on a bull-hide shield; upon its face was painted an angry bull with bloody horns lowering his head to make an attack.

" 'Father, why are making a shield when you already have one?' I asked.

"After a short time of silence he answered without looking up from his work, 'I am making this shield for you, my son, and the angry bull painted upon it shall be your individual totem, a warrior's totem.' He then held the shield up at arm's length and examined it to satisfy himself of its style and beauty. When, after a few touches, it was finished, he laid it gently upon a bear skin spread on the ground in the back part of the teepee.

" 'But, father, why don't you hang it up on a pole outside in front of the teepee as you do yours?' I said.

"Again there was a long silence and the old man said, 'My son, that is for you to do. Every warrior must hang up his own shield. Ordinarily it is an act so easily performed that it may be done by any woman or child, but the weight of it is so great, in what it signifies, that it requires a heart that has the strength of courage, a heart that shrinks not from danger, to raise it from the ground of obscurity. He who displays this emblem of valor without first winning that right shall deservedly draw upon himself the scorn and derision of men. This shield must, therefore, stay upon the ground until you lift it up with the strong hand of valor, truly tested upon the field of battle. It is the custom among our people for a warrior to challenge the son of another warrior to some valorous deed, by presenting him with a spear, a shield, or a war bonnet. No one, my son, seems to care to do us that honor, so I do it myself.' The old man said much more about valor and honor and emblems, but my thoughts dwelt upon the game I had partly won, and while he was yet speaking, I arose and hastened to the play grounds.

"One bright morning as an interesting game was in progress, there was a sudden cry of alarm. In an instant the camp was in the wildest confusion. The great herds of horses thundered toward camp in a mad stampede. The men at play threw down their javelins and they, as well as the spectators, hastily slung their quivers over their shoulders and ran for their horses, and I was left alone on the play grounds. For no special purpose or definite plan of action, I walked toward my home as though nothing was happening. Already the warriors, armed and decked for battle, were galloping out of camp, cheered by the women with death songs and cries of the bird-hawk, that bird of dauntless courage. My father was waiting for me at the door. He held my horse by the bit with one hand while with the other he offered me my lance. I liked not the looks of the horse. He fiercely pounded the earth with his hoofs and with loud snorts pranced around the old man as though mad.

" 'Mount!' shouted my father, in stern command, as I reluctantly grasped the lance.

" 'But father, where is my shield?' I asked, dodging the hoofs of the frantic horse.

" 'When have you shown us that you need a shield?' he replied in a tone of contempt. 'Hurry and mount!'

"I still stood hesitating. Then happened the ridiculous that sometimes happens in a moment most critical. A frowzy-headed girl who, like others, was watching the warriors gallop by called out, 'Oh, mother, look at O-be-ska. He is going out to dig wild potatoes!' " (a woman's occupation).

At this, the wife of the aged warrior who sat among the listeners turned her head aside and chuckled to herself as she smoothed her hair with her crooked fingers.

"Stung to a sudden decision by that taunt of the impudent

girl," continued the old man, "I grasped the horse by the mane and at a single bound sprang upon his bare back. He leaped forward and sped away as swiftly as the wind. He needed no urging or guiding as he struck for the dark trail made by the warriors hastening to meet the foe.

"The army gathered upon a high hill. A man with a war bonnet trailing to the ground and mounted on a coal-black horse raised his hand and shouted, 'There they come, but dismount and give the horses a little time to breathe. When they come to yonder point, we will make the test charge.'

"The warriors dismounted and, pulling handsful of grass, brushed the foam from the sides of the panting horses. Then they set to work to test the soundness of their bows and strings.

"I did not dismount but sat gazing in the direction where the leader had pointed. The only thing that I could see was a yellowish cloud in the distance rising in the air. I looked below the line of the hills, and there came the enemy. They blackened the side of the hill, beyond the valley, as they approached us at an easy canter. They came to the point indicated by the man with the trailing war bonnet.

" 'E-hu!' shouted the leader as with the easy grace of a lynx he vaulted upon the back of his horse.

"In an instant every man was mounted, the horses sprang forward, and we charged down the grassy slope with the speed of the whirlwind and rending the air with the battle cry. My horse carried me among the fleetest. I was at the extreme end of the line at the right. We came within arrow shot of the foe when suddenly our army swung to the left like a great flock of birds. I pulled the reins and leaned heavily to the left to follow. The horse yielded his head and neck as willingly as the willow sapling; his ear touched my naked breast, but he rushed madly on.

"The arrows whizzed like angry bees around me, and before I knew what was happening, I dashed into the line of the enemy and came with a crash against a horse and his rider. The two beasts reared upon their hind legs. I could see the warrior's clenched teeth gleam between his parted lips. Something flashed from among the feathers and fringes of his jacket, and a sharp pain suddenly shot through my breast. I fell to the ground but arose in an instant. Then there came a noise like the loud rumbling of thunder. Just then something struck my head, and a darkness blacker than any night came over me.

"While yet in that awful darkness there came to me sounds like that of a drum, as though from a distance. It came nearer and nearer; then I heard the voices of men and of women joined in a song of victory. The drum ceased, the voices alone carried the song, and in the wild cadences I heard my own name, followed by words of praise. I opened my eyes, and a man who was sitting near me exclaimed: 'It is done. He lives!' And he rubbed the palms of his hands in happy triumph. It was the medicine man.

"For a long time I lay silent, wondering what had happened. The front of the tent had been thrown open. At the left of the entrance stood a pole upon which hung a new shield, its bright trimmings and feathers swaying gently in the breeze.

"My father, seeing that my eyes were fixed intently upon the piece of bull-hide that meant so much to him, spoke with unconcealed pride, 'That is your shield, my son,' he said. 'You have won the right to display it and to wear it when you go to do your part in the defense of your people against their enemies.'

"As my father was speaking, all that I had seen in that battle came back to my mind with sudden clearness. I then knew there was some mistake, some misunderstanding. I made an effort to explain. 'My horse went so fast I couldn't—'

"'Lie still,' commanded the medicine man. 'You will start afresh the bleeding of the wound.'

"One bright morning, in the fall of that year, when all the people had returned to the permanent village, I heard the voice of the crier calling to the warriors to gather at the long tent prepared by the War clan and receive their badges of honor upon proof of the right to them. There was a stir throughout the village, and men, women, and children flocked toward the long tent, all eager to see the public awarding of honors to the braves who exposed themselves to the dangers of battle and won distinction in defending the camp. I lay sick from my wound that had refused to heal, so I could not go although I longed to see the ceremonies. Soon I heard the booming of the drum and then the voices of the war priests giving the chant to the Thunder-gods who controlled the wars and battles and decided the fate of the warrior. Then I heard the voice of one priest reciting the ritual in which the aspirant for war honors is solemnly adjured to follow the path of truth and warned against speaking falsely in telling his story, for if he should attempt to deceive the Thunder-gods, he would surely be struck by lightning, be bitten by a poisonous snake, or be gored to death by an angry bull. The ritual came to an end. Then the warrior, in a voice bold and clear, recited his story. There came a pause and then a sudden outburst of the wildest cheering by the men and women. So it went on until I fell asleep to dream of lightning, snakes, and angry bulls.

"When I awoke, the people of the house had returned and in a lively manner were discussing the ceremonies of the day, laughing heartily at the blunders of some of the younger warriors and praising the calm and dignified bearing of the older ones.

"My father came in, and as he sat down by my side, he handed me an eagle feather, saying as he did so, 'They have given you this decoration. You are to wear it standing upright in your scalplock. It means that you have struck an enemy in a hand-to-hand fight. Besides this they have given you the privilege of painting an outspread hand on your naked chest at the dances of the society of The Braves, should you become a member. That means that you were struck by an enemy. These two high honors they have awarded you. They have also thrown away your boy name and given you the name Wa-ha-ton-ga, the ancient name for shield. A friend made your claim for you.'

"I have often wondered which of the two, my friend or I, was to suffer those awful penalties, but since his death by drowning it became certain to me that I am the one to be tossed by an angry bull.

"But from that day to this I have never even witnessed a game of hoop and javelin, and since then my constant companions have been the lance and shield."

"Grandmother," said a young girl who had been listening

intently to the story. "What for did you make fun of my grandfather like that?"

"Te he," chuckled the old woman. "He stood there so handsome and good for nothing, I thought it might help his father make him go to the battle."

Ta-de'-win

Omaha ethnographies describe various practices related to courtship and marriage, including those that make up the subject of this story. A two-page manuscript titled "Ta-dae-win" in La Flesche's papers in the Smithsonian Institution was apparently written at a different time than the text reprinted here and may have been intended as a framework for this story.

CEASE FOR A MOMENT YOUR pleasures, my young brothers, and listen to the story of an old man. Let the fire burn brightly so that I may look into your faces and know that you hear my words.

Long, long ago, on a summer night when the camp of the Le-hi-da lay in the great bend of the Turbid [Missouri] River, a place well known to you all, I stood in the shadow of a tent with my arms clasped about the slender form of a young woman. Patches of clouds swept over the growing moon, and people passed to and fro. All were bent upon their own affairs, so that we two were left unmolested. Lifting her face up to mine, the young woman whispered, "I love you and all my life I shall follow you as my husband, and no one shall take me from you. If I speak not true then let a violent death come upon me." My heart thrilled with joy. At last I had won after a long wooing. I pressed the little body close to my breast and kissed her lips because I had for her a true love and I honored her.

There was a movement within the tent, and a woman's voice in a tone full of tenderness arose, "Wino$^{n'}$,[1] the damp air and the dew are not good for you; hasten and come in." I released the young woman, and she was gone.

On the following day I spoke to my father and mother of the exchange of promises I had made with the young woman to marry, and in hearing her name their faces brightened with gladness, for they knew she was of a family that had the respect of all good people. She, too, had made known to her parents my proposal and her acceptance of me, and they had given their approval. And thus it came about that one day messengers selected by my father passed, with great show of solemnity, back and forth between the tents of our parents to procure the formal consent of both families to the marriage.

The news spread rapidly, and soon old and young were talking of the coming marriage between pretty Ta-de'-win and the young O-mon'-hon [Omaha]. Many expressed the opinion that we were well suited to each other, while some said, "She should have chosen a man from her own tribe."

Never before, nor since that time, had my patience been put to a test so severe. The formalities seemed to me to be endlessly long, but the older people (to maintain a proper dignity) took particular care not to give the slightest appearance of anxious haste, so there was nothing for me to do but wait and wait.

The messengers returned to my father's tent, delivered their final message, took their fees, and went to their homes. The marriage was to take place on the morrow. The sun was slower than the messengers. Anxiously, I watched it until at last it disappeared behind the hills, and then night came, a night that brought me neither sleep nor dreams and passed even slower than did the sun.

Morning came, then the sun into a cloudless sky. It was a good omen, and I thank the gods for brightening the day of my marriage. I arose and hastily ate the food placed before me by my mother; then at her bidding I put on new clothing that I might appear well at the ceremony. Suddenly, a woman nearby exclaimed, "Oh, look, they're coming!"

The pulsations of my heart quickened, and I could hardly restrain myself from running to the door to see if it was true, but my father and mother sat motionless and showed no signs of excitement. There was a murmur of voices around us; then a number of footsteps approached rapidly, and the front of our tent was quickly unlaced and the sides like wings thrown apart and fastened to poles planted firmly in the ground by my three girl cousins. Then I could see, sure enough, the procession led by Ta-de'-win was slowly approaching our tent. When she came within a throwing distance, the three young women ran forward and spread on the ground before her a large robe upon which they made her sit; then grasping the edges, they lifted her and carried her into our tent and placed her by my side. Then followed her father and mother and all her near relatives, who were greeted by my father and assigned to seats according to the degrees of kinship. My cousins brought their tent and added it to ours to make more room for the guests.

For a long while my father sat in silence, and when at last he lifted his head to make his address to Ta-de'-win's father, in acknowledgment of the great honor conferred upon his house, everyone became silent.

That was still a part of the ceremony. My father brought in three of our best horses, and when my wife stepped out of the tent to go and make her visit, he put the lariats in her hands, and she led them to her father's tent. In a few days my wife came home, bringing with her three of her father's horses, and this concluded the marriage rite.

All this took place when the two tribes were on the summer hunt. When the hunt was over, the two tribes separated, the O-mon'-hon going to their own home and the Le-hi-da to theirs.

NOTE

1. *Wino^n*, meaning "my eldest," was a term used by either her father or her mother to address the eldest daughter who was grown. See Fletcher and La Flesche, *The Omaha Tribe*, 317.

The Captive Maid

This story is unusual in this collection because it is about Pawnees. La Flesche had a broad range of resources concerning the Pawnees to draw upon for the story: the traditional history of the Omahas; his father, who knew the Pawnees through trading with them; his knowledge of J. Owen Dorsey's work on the Pawnees; and his acquaintance with James Murie, the Pawnee who served as an informant for Alice C. Fletcher. Pawnee orthography and translations are provided by Martha Royce Blaine.

MANY YEARS AGO, LONG BEFORE the valleys and the prairies west of the Missouri were ever marked by the plow of the white man, the Pawnee village with its dome-shaped earth lodges lay along the south bank of the river Platte, not far from its confluence with the Loup. On a summer morning, at break of day, while the village was still in silent slumber, a boy came out of the long entranceway of one of the peculiar dwellings. He paused as he felt the cool air, yawned, stretched himself, looked for a moment at the sky, and then approached a corral nearby. He unfastened the bars, and one by one the horses confined within walked out. He drove the hungry animals to a hill overlooking the village and then stood watching them as they busily fed upon the grass laden with dew.

As the sun peeped over the eastern horizon, there began to

be signs of life in the village below. Smoke curled upward from the tops of the houses, then singly and in groups the women and girls hastened toward the river to get the morning supply of water while the men and boys released the horses from the corrals and drove them to the pastures among the hills. Last to come out was Ke-wa-gu [Ki-wa-ku, Fox], a frowzy-headed boy of some thirteen or fourteen years. He was in a rebellious mood because his mother, brought to the end of her patience by his laziness, had dragged him out of his bed and driven him to his work. He unfastened the bars of the corral and threw them to the ground with considerable violence, and as the lean, sore-backed, shrinking horses came out, he gave each one a vicious whack with a heavy quirt. When the hungry beasts came to the edge of the village, they began to devour the tops of the weeds, and there the sullen boy left them to shift for themselves while he went on up the hill. Every little while he tossed a captive bird up into the air and laughed a wicked laugh as he jerked it back with a long string to which it was tied. At the top of the hill he discovered the boy who had risen earlier than all the rest to let his horses feed in the cool of the morning when the flies are not so troublesome.

Recognizing his next-door neighbor, Ke-wa-gu, holding aloft the fluttering captive, called out, "Ta-ra-ha [Buffalo], see what I've got!"

Ta-ra-ha looked up and saw the little meadow lark bravely struggling to release itself from its captor. "Bring here the bird," he said, "and give it to me."

"Gaw-gee [Kah-ki, no]," replied Ke-wa-gu, shaking his unkempt head and putting the bird behind his back. "I do not want to give it to you."

Ta-ra-ha, reaching down into his quiver, drew from it an arrow and held it up temptingly to Ke-wa-gu.

As his eyes fell upon the mottled feathers and the bright colorings of the shaft, the sullen expression that had distorted Ke-wa-gu's childish features relaxed and a smile of real pleasure spread over his face. He surrendered the bird and grasped the arrow, and the trade was done.

While Ke-wa-gu was examining his treasure with happy pride, Ta-ra-ha hastily unfastened the string from the leg of the bird and then with a graceful movement tossed it up into the air. As though uncertain of its freedom, the bird at first flew around in a circle, and then it shot forth with the swiftness of the wind, singing to itself.

Ke-wa-gu started as though to pursue, but Ta-ra-ha quickly caught him by the belt and stopped him, and the two stood watching with wondering interest the flight of the happy creature. It sped over the river in an undulating motion, now up and now down, a habit peculiar to its kind, over the low hills beyond, until its form diminished in the distance in a tiny speck and then finally vanished in the great blue sky.

"It has gone home to Te-ra-wa [Ti-ra-wa], the God of the Sky," said Ta-ra-ha gravely, as though speaking to himself, and he gently released his hold of Ke-wa-gu's belt.

In the excitement of the barter Ke-wa-gu altogether lost sight of the fact that an arrow without a bow had but little value and that he had none that he could call his own. This he did not realize until he thought to try the weapon, and then shyly he approached Ta-ra-ha and said, "E-ra-re [I-ra-ri, brother], I have no bow. Will you lend me yours?"

"I rather not," replied Ta-ra-ha, and he walked toward home, where a breakfast of hot hominy and a bowl of pemmican awaited him.

Part Two

Stories of Tradition

The Twins and Two-Face

This story is based on a traditional Omaha tale, "Two-Faces and the Twin Brothers," an incomplete version of which Dorsey collected and translated. La Flesche left several manuscripts relating to the story. A manuscript fragment, which he may have intended to incorporate into the story, is among his papers in the Smithsonian Institution. It closely follows the lines of the traditional story as it explains in more detail how the twins' mother died from having looked at Two-Face after she had been warned not to do so. In the traditional story, Two-Faces cut the woman open, left one twin, but took the other and left him for the wild mice to raise. La Flesche left another version of the story, titled "The Twin Brothers' Adventures," preserved in the La Flesche family papers in the Nebraska State Historical Society. In it, the twin boys remain with their father, but one soon apparently dies, and the father wraps him in a buffalo robe and hides his body in a hollow tree. But the child is not really dead and survives because the mice bring him wild beans to eat. Meanwhile, the father feeds the child who remains with him on soup. Hence the song about soup and beans. The version reprinted here, which appears to be La Flesche's last, exists partly in holograph and partly in typescript in La Flesche's papers in the Smithsonian Institution.

ALL DRIPPING WITH THE MORNING's dew The-Little-Wild-One stood on a grassy knoll looking down on a solitary teepee among the woods below. He whistled loudly, but there was no response; no head was thrust out of the top of the door flap to see what the whistle call meant. Then The-Little-Wild-One lifted his child voice and sang:

Wi i tha da un thin ga gun, hin blthin aha
bltha ta a thin ha
Thi i tha da tha tun ga ta nu za nun tha shin
Ta nu za nun tun tha thin sha.

I have no father, so I live on wild beans
I live on wild beans
You have a father, so you live on soup
You live on soup.[1]

Four little fingers were cautiously thrust out of the top of the door flap, and through the small opening made by the fingers, two twinkling eyes peeped to look for the singer. The sharp eyes of The-Little-Wild-One saw the fingers thrust out to open a crack at the top of the door flap and the questioning eyes that peeped through and he called, "Is your father at home?" The door flap was quickly pushed aside and out came a little boy about his own size and just like himself in appearance.

"Is your father at home?" repeated The-Little-Wild-One, in a half-suspicious tone.

"No, my father's gone a-hunting," replied little Forget. "Come down and play with me."

With a hop and a skip The-Little-Wild-One ran down the hill and in cautious manner peered into the door of the teepee. Then suddenly forgetting his fears, he exclaimed, "Oh, what joy! Can I eat some of those?" pointing to a row of skewers that stood all around the fire-place and [were] loaded with bits of roasted venison, tempting to hungry mouths.

"Yes," shouted Forget, all excited. "Let's sit down and eat, and then we'll play all day long."

The two sat down and ate and ate with smacking of lips

and licking of fingers until they could eat no more. Then they romped in and out of the teepee and played at hide-and-seek and wrestled until there remained no sign of tidiness in and about the teepee and both were all out of breath.

"Tell me who you are," said Forget with startling suddenness as they sat down to rest. "I never saw you before."

"Don't ask me who I am," whispered The-Little-Wild-One, with a look of alarm. "If you do, I'll go away and never come back any more."

"Don't go 'way," pleaded Forget. "I won't ask you that again, but tell me, what's outside of this teepee, way off yonder among those dark woods? I've never been outside of this teepee, away from this fire-place with its curling smoke. Tell me everything."

"Doesn't your father let you go anywheres at all?" asked The-Little-Wild-One in a voice full of sympathy. "I don't think it's nice at all, because if you don't go anywheres, you will never know anything."

"Tell me all you know," begged Forget, "of the things in the woods. I want to know about them."

"Sit very still, then," said The-Little-Wild-One, "and listen, and I will tell you. Do you ever hear a voice like this at night, Oo, oo, oo-oo, Oo, oo, oo-oo?"

"Yes," replied Forget, "and I get very scared."

"That is Wa-poo-ga, the [barred] owl," continued The-Little-Wild-One, "and he is one of the meanest of birds. He has a crooked beak like that (bending his forefinger), and great big eyes like that (making a ring with his thumb and finger), and two tufts of feathers on his head standing out from his ears, and he has claws as sharp as thorns. At night when it is very dark, he goes about and snatches the sleeping mice from their nests and eats them up. He eats other birds, too, and that's why I don't like him at all. Hark! Do you hear that rapping sound? That's Moopa [red-headed woodpecker], the smartest and happiest of birds. He has white and black wings and bright red feathers on his head. As he flies through the air in that up-and-down motion of his, going from tree to tree, he shouts with joy. He makes his home in a hollow tree, and he feeds on the caterpillars and worms that nest in the bark. He has ears that can hear anything and a bill as hard as stone. When he has picked all the worms from the bark of a tree, he goes to a dead one and he listens, moves on, and listens until he hears a worm gnawing his way deep inside of the hard wood, and he pounds away with his bill till he gets the worm. That's what he was doing when you heard him."

All day long The-Little-Wild-One sat and described to his companion the lives and the habits of other birds, skillfully imitating the song and cry of each bird as he spoke, and Forget sat with chin resting in the palm of his hand and eyes fixed upon the little stranger, listening with ever increasing interest. The sun touched the western hills and was sinking behind them when suddenly The-Little-Wild-One sprang to his feet, tapped with the tips of his fingers the head of his companion, uttering the word FORGET and then fled as though from some approaching danger.

Soon after the flight of The-Little-Wild-One the father came home, and seeing the robes and other articles of the teepee lying about in disorder, he said, "How is this? Everything is disarranged; and look at the fire-place, it is most untidy. And what has become of all the roast venison? There was enough to feed two boys, and it is all gone. Has anyone been here?"

"Oh, yes, father!" exclaimed Forget. "There was a — "

"What?" asked the father. "Anybody?"

"I forget," replied the boy vacantly.

Before break of day the hunter rose, kindled the fire, replenished the skewers around the fire-place with fresh venison, and started out while Forget still lay dreaming under his raccoon-skin robe.

The sun was peeping over the tops of the hills and the trees when The-Little-Wild-One again stood on the knoll and whistled to the lonely teepee below. When there came no response, he sang his little song of wild beans and sweet juices of meat, and then the door flap flew high into the air and out came Forget, calling excitedly, "Come on, come on down and play with me!"

"Is your father at home?" asked The-Little-Wild-One, suspiciously.

"No," replied Forget. "My father's gone a-hunting; hurry down and play with me."

"Sure he's gone?" asked The-Little-Wild-One, doubtfully. "What's that dark thing way back there?"

"That's my father's robe, all rolled up. Hurry down here and don't be so 'fraid."

The-Little-Wild-One entered the teepee, touched the robe cautiously with his foot, peered behind the row of packs, and when he was quite sure that the hunter had really gone, he sat down and feasted on roast venison with his little host. When the skewers were nearly all stripped of the meat, Forget said, "You have told me of the creatures that have wings and fly in the air and make their homes in the trees; now tell me of the four-footed creatures that live on and in the ground."

"There are about as many kinds as the birds," replied The-Little-Wild-One, "and as different in their ways of living and getting their food. I like them all, but I like best Zha-bae, the beavers, because they are the smartest of them all. Their food is the bark of the trees, and their homes are always along the banks of a stream. When they have selected a good place for their village, they set to work cutting trees down to store away the limbs for their winter food and to use for the frames of their houses. They cut the trees with their teeth, which are as sharp as any knife can be. Sometimes one, sometimes two, and sometimes three work at a tree. When the part that they are cutting gets to be very small, they know that they have to look out for their lives, so one of them reaches up and puts his paw on the trunk of the tree above the cut place, and when he feels the tree going, he scampers behind the stump as do the rest, and down comes the tree with a crash. Then begins the work of cutting the limbs. They cut them in lengths about twice the length of my arms spread out, and they drag them to the stream, where they plant them in the mud under the water all the way across the stream. The work goes on without stopping until the pile of limbs gets thicker and thicker and higher and higher, and it chokes up the stream, and the water gets very deep above the pile of tree limbs, which becomes their winter feeding place.

While some are hard at work storing away the limbs, others

are busy dragging poles to the sites chosen for the houses. The
houses are built just above the water's edge along the banks, and
in the center of each is a hole that goes slanting down, down to
the water, and that is the way the beavers go in and out of their
houses, to and from their feeding place. The beavers, like all
other animals, have something to be afraid of, so when they are
at home in their house, and they hear a noise outside which they
think is the thing they are afraid of, they rush to this hole, and
down they go with a swish! and out into the deep water where
they are safe. I wish you could see them. To know them one
should see them."

"I wish I could see them and all the other things you tell
about," said little Forget, who sat and listened in his usual
attentive attitude, "but I never can get away from this place."

Willing to tell of the life with which he was so closely associated and having a willing listener, which pleased him equally
well, The-Little-Wild-One went on with his stories, all unconscious of the passing of the day until the sun was setting red
beyond the western hills, when, startled by some noise, he suddenly sprang to his feet and fled with such haste that he forgot to
put the forget spell on his companion which he had been doing.
And so it was that as soon as the hunter came home and stooped
to enter the teepee, little Forget, being free of the bewildering
spell, shouted out, "Oh, father! There's been a little boy here and
played with me all day long, and he told me all about the owl and
the woodpecker and the beaver and many other things that you
never tell me about. He comes here as soon as you go away in the
morning."

"You have found your brother whom I have been hunting for

these many winters," said the man thoughtfully. "When Two-Face killed your mother, he left you by her side, but he carried your brother away. He has come back, though wild like the birds and the beasts among whom he has lived. We must catch him and in this way: Tomorrow when he comes, you must offer to braid his long hair as yours is. When you have done so, wind the braided locks tightly around your right hand and call to me. I shall lie hid nearby and come quickly when you call."

Again as the sun spread its morning light over the eastern hills, The-Little-Wild-One came as before and stood on the grassy knoll and sang his song of wild beans and the sweet juices of meat.

"Hurry down here and let's play," shouted Forget as he rushed out, tossing the door flap aside.

"Is your father at home?" asked The-Little-Wild-One in a tone full of distrust.

"My father's gone a-hunting. Hurry down and play with me," said Forget persuasively.

"Lift up the side of the teepee and let me look in," said The-Little-Wild-One, more distrustful than ever. "I feel your father nearby."

"My father's not here," replied Forget, hurriedly pulling some of the pegs and lifting high the side of the teepee. "He's gone a-hunting."

"I'll come down," said The-Little-Wild-One, his little heart thumping wildly, "though I still feel your father nearby, and if he's really gone, we'll play."

The-Little-Wild-One started down the hill, not with his

confident hop and a skip, but slowly and cautiously. The movement of a crooked stick he trod on startled him. He entered the teepee, and the two had their feast of roast venison, and they romped and wrestled as before, and when they were both out of breath, they sat down while The-Little-Wild-One told of the lives and habits of the birds and imitated their songs and cries.

"Let me braid your hair like mine," suggested Forget. "It will look better and not be so much in your way."

The-Little-Wild-One consented, forgetting all fears, and Forget worked away at the braid while his companion chatted in a lively way about the birds whom he loved dearly. When the long lock was braided, Forget very slyly wrapped it around his right hand and then called out, "Father, I've caught him, come quick!"

The-Little-Wild-One struggled with all his might, but the father rushed in and quickly cut the long braided lock and the little boy ceased struggling.

After the loss of his lock The-Little-Wild-One was content to stay in his new home and never tried to get away. So little Forget had a brother, a companion to play with while his father was gone on his hunts.

To make the little fellow forget the loss of his lock the father made for him an artificial one which was so long that it hung way down to his waist. From the base to the tip the man ornamented the lock with pretty shell disks graduating in size all the way down. The little fellow danced with joy, and Forget secretly envied his brother.

One day the hunter said to the brothers, "Tomorrow I shall

go hunting. The meat is nearly gone, and you will go hungry. Do not go away from the teepee but stay near it, and when you get hungry, eat the meat roasting on the skewers. Do not go to that black forest over yonder, or you will get lost. Do not go there."

Before the sun arose and [while] the little ones were still sound asleep, the hunter took his bow and arrows and went out to hunt for deer. It was broad day when the boys awoke, and they sat down to eat their breakfast of roast venison. While they were eating, little Forget said to his brother, "Friend, let me wear your scalp lock today, won't you?"

"Yes," said The-Little-Wild-One, "but you must let me have it tomorrow. I want to wear it myself."

When breakfast was over, the boys raced and romped around the teepee, but The-Little-Wild-One was not as lively as he used to be. When they sat down to rest, he looked toward the forest that lay dark and mysterious in the distance. Forget plucked at his brother's arm to make him play, but The-Little-Wild-One said, "Friend, let us go over to that big forest where your father told us not to go."

"No, I don't want to go," replied Forget, for before this he was an obedient little boy, and he did not want to displease his father. "My father told us not to."

"Then give me back my scalp lock," said The-Little-Wild-One angrily, "and I'll go away and never come back again."

"Don't go away," said Forget in alarm. "I'll go with you."

The two started out, and when the sun got up to the middle of heaven, they entered the forest and wandered about among the big trees. The trees were larger and taller than any they had ever seen. Nothing happened to them until they came to a large cedar tree. It was bare of branches except at the top. Among those branches there was a huge nest made of broken branches of trees and strips of bark.

"That's an awful big nest," said Forget. "I wonder what kind of birds they are."

"I'll go up and see," said The-Little-Wild One. "You stay down here."

The-Little-Wild-One hugged the trunk of the tree with his arms and knees and climbed slowly up. When he mounted the edge of the nest, there burst forth a roar of thunder amid flashes of lightning.

"They're thunder-birds," yelled The-Little-Wild-One to his brother. "I'm going to throw them down one by one. You get a big stick and whack them. Don't kill them, but just stun them."

One by one The-Little-Wild-One threw the birds down and Forget gave each one a whack with a big stick. Each one gave a little kick and then [lay] stunned.

"Your father will be very glad," said The-Little-Wild-One when he came to the ground. "These birds will make fine pets."

When the boys entered the teepee, the birds recovered from the blows they had received, and they struggled to get free, but they were tied securely to the teepee poles, where they sat blinking out flashes of lightning.

The boys waited outside for their father to come home, and when they heard him coming at dusk, they ran in and poked the birds with sharp sticks and made them roar with thunder, and the teepee was filled with flashes of lightning.

"What's all this?" said the father as he bent low to enter the teepee. "Didn't I tell you not to go to the black forest? Now go tie those birds to the trees outside and tomorrow carry them back to their nest."

Some few days passed when the hunter again told the twins that he would go hunting, for the meat was again nearly gone. The three stood outside near the door of the teepee and from where they stood they could see far away in the distance a high cliff wrapped in bluish haze. "Do not go to yonder cliff," warned the hunter again and again. He knew the perversity of the young minds, knew that they would do the very opposite of what he desired. He wished them to go to the mysterious forest, dark and black, and the surest way to have them go was to tell them most earnestly not to go. He knew that there they would unwittingly get magic which he wished them to have for a single purpose. And now he wished them to go to the mysterious cliff veiled in bluish haze, and he used the surest way to have them go. Before the rise of sun the hunter stole out of his teepee while the twins still lay dreaming under their little raccoon-skin robes.

The sun touched the hills and trees with its early rays and then shot a stream of light into the teepee through a tiny hole on the east side. "The sun is coming in," shouted The-Little-Wild-One. "Let's get up, you lazy boy."

Up sprang Forget, and both raced to the little stream that raced through the woods not far away, and both with shouts and laughter splashed among the tumbling waters till all feeling of drowsiness was clean gone. Then back to the teepee the two hastened and feasted upon the bits of venison that merrily sizzled upon the skewers around the fire.

Then began the rompings and wrestling; in and out of the teepee the two chased each other in boisterous fashion, till all of a sudden The-Little-Wild-One stopped and said to Forget almost in a whisper, "Let's go to that cliff over yonder, where your father told us not to go."

"But my father told us not to go," was the quick reply of the stay-at-home.

"Then give me back my lock," cried The-Little-Wild-One with a pout.

"I was just fooling; I'll go with you," said Forget, grasping tightly the much coveted lock.

On a jog trot the two struck out, looking neither to the right nor to the left nor behind. They came to the base of the cliff and stopped to look at the jagged rocks far above their little heads and to watch the swallows that busily flew in and out of their mud-plaster nests, some with excited calls and others with soothing, gurgling sounds. The nests were glued to the smooth rocks far out of the reach of the twins, and they stood wondering how they could get to them, when with startling suddenness there arose rattling sounds at their very feet. The youngsters quickly looked down, and there were the rattlers all around them, some stretched out on the grass, and others coiled on the loose stones that lay scattered about, and their skins glistened in the sun.

"Oh, what beauties!" cried The-Little-Wild-One with a clap of his hands. "Get a stick; let's cut off their tails!"

The two, armed with sticks, set to work pressing the heads of the wriggling snakes to the ground and cutting their tails off with stone knives.

"Go for those that are lying straight; don't go near those coiled up," warned The-Little-Wild-One. "And take the biggest ones; they have the longest tails."

With mingled feelings of pleasure and pride, the two little adventurers entered their teepee and chose at once the door flap as the most suitable place for the display of their trophies. Both set to work with awl and sinew sewing the rattles to the door flap. Every bit of the flap from top to bottom was covered with rattles when the work was done; then in and out the twins ran to try the effect of the sound, and both clapped their hands and shouted in glee at the success.

When the sun was sinking in the west The-Little-Wild-One said to his brother, "Friend, I feel your father coming home; let's go in and sit down and wait and see what he will do when he raises the door flap to come in." Both went into the teepee and waited in silence. Soon the father came. He lifted the door flap, bent low, and entered, and the flap came down with the crash of many rattles. The-Little-Wild-One and Forget put their hands to their mouths to suppress the giggles, and the father, with feigned displeasure, said, "What disobedient children you are! Did I not tell you not to go near that cliff! Go, tomorrow, and return the rattles to those snakes. You have deprived them of their magic!"

By the touch of the thunder-birds and the rattlers The-Little-Wild-One and Forget had absorbed magic. They had become possessed of the same power possessed by Two-Face, who killed their mother. They were now ready with equal strength to meet and battle with the destroyer; so on a certain day The-Little-

Wild-One said to his father, "Tell us now where this Two-Face lives so that we, Forget and I, may go and destroy him as he has destroyed our mother."

"Far off toward the rising sun, in an island in the middle of a great lake, dwells Two-Face, the destroyer," replied the father. "His magic is so great that no human being can destroy him."

"Make a canoe for us," said The-Little-Wild-One, "and we, Forget and I, will go and destroy Two-Face."

Out of the trunk of a tree the father built a canoe and made paddles for it out of an ash, a magical tree. On both sides of the bow and stern of the canoe he carved the four thunder-birds and along the body the rattlers, in lines, all stiff, angular, and fantastic, and the canoe was done. Before break of day it was launched in the stream that ran through the woods nearby, and The-Little-Wild-One and Forget paddled swiftly away. And when the sun was up high, they shot into the great blue lake. Four days and four nights they paddled, and they came in sight of the island where dwelt Two-Face, the destroyer. By his magic, Two-Face felt the coming of The-Little-Wild-One and Forget, and he became afraid, for he knew that they had magical power and could fight him with equal strength. To prevent their landing he set in motion the waters around the island so that the waves dashed up high in the air and tumbled down in rolling turmoil. The two paddled all the harder and the canoe, carried by a high wave, shot forward and landed safely far upon the dry beach. Then the battle began on land amidst a heavy cloud and flashes of fire and poisoned arrows. The island trembled with the noise of thunder. Four days and four nights passed with ceaseless fighting, and then Two-Face fell. The-Little-Wild-One and Forget gathered dried branches of trees and, piling them upon the body, burned it to ashes. But when they started to leave, Two-Face suddenly rose up out of the ashes, and the battle began again more furious than before. Four more days and nights passed with ceaseless fighting when again Two-Face fell. Then The-Little-Wild-One and Forget drew fire from the sky with which they burned the body of Two-Face, and he was utterly destroyed.

NOTE

1. La Flesche left space in the typescript of this story to insert the song. The song reprinted here is taken from his manuscript "The Twin Brothers' Adventures."

The Spring, the Mischief Maker,
and the Tree

In this little story, La Flesche draws on a common motif in folk literatures — the mischief maker who becomes entrapped or "stuck" as a result of his own rash or foolhardy actions. One major difference, however, is that the mischief maker is also often the trickster, who uses his wits to escape. Here, the mischief maker displays no characteristics of the trickster and is punished for his actions that endanger the tribe.

A N INDIAN TRIBE TRAVELED VERY far in search of buffalo and other game. In their travel they came to a country where there was no water; for several days they continued without water, suffering from thirst, as did also their little ones. At last they came in sight of a river, the banks of which were studded with forests. Approaching the river, they found the bed dry; up and down they walked, and then young and old began to dig into the sand until exhausted. Soon a young man dug with his hands, and after much effort he saw water bubbling up from the bottom of the hole that he had dug. He tasted it and found it cold and sweet; as he drank of this water, his strength was revived.

Close to this spring a tree stood with outspreading limbs, which threw a cool shade over it. The young man shouted with gladness, calling loudly to the people. They came quickly; the children were allowed to drink first, then all dipped their vessels and drank and were strengthened. While they lingered about the great spring in the shade, game came; thus they secured food at this place.

One morning, greatly to their dismay, they found the spring filled up and closed with sand. Examination discovered that a man had done the malicious work with his heels and foot. This was again done. This time the mark of footprints were left by the man. It was now time for the people to find out who the guilty one was and punish him, if possible, the mischief maker, feeling sure the act would be repeated. About the middle of the night following, the wicked man appeared and began his malicious work, but as he started, he heard a kind of clicking sound as made by a tongue issuing from the tree. This made the man angry; turning to the tree, he said, "If you do that again, I will strike you with my fist." Again he started to work, again he heard the same sound. As he had threatened, so he struck the tree, but his hand stuck fast. He pulled and pulled; still he stuck. Then he struck the tree with his left hand. This he could not loosen. Then he kicked the tree with his left foot; that also stuck. By this time the man was very angry and said, "I now have only my forehead to strike you with; if you do not let me go, I will use it." The tree replied, "Strike." So the man struck the tree with his forehead; it also stuck to the tree.

Very early in the morning a woman came to the sacred spring for water. She beheld the wicked man stuck to the tree. Lifting her voice, she called to the people telling them the bad man was caught. When the men pulled him away, he was dead. The tree had punished him.

He-ba-cha-ge and Sin-de-dum-pa

This story is La Flesche's variation on an Omaha story, "The Buffalo and the Grizzly Bear." In the version collected by J. Owen Dorsey, Grizzly Bear attacks Buffalo Bull three times, each time grabbing him by the hair of his head, the horns, or the tail, but each time ending the attack by striking him in the scrotum with the flat of his paw. Only after the third attack does Buffalo Bull decide to retaliate. La Flesche may have glossed the details of the attack, by having the bear slap the buffalo in the face, out of deference to the genteel sensibilities of youthful American readers at the turn of the century.

O N THE SUNNY SIDE OF A HILL sat He-ba-cha-ge, Blunt-horns, dozing and dreaming, perhaps of the younger days of his life when, by his great strength and courage, he made himself master and lord of a goodly-sized herd. He maintained his mastery of the herd so long as his physical strength endured, but there came a time when a stranger appeared who, after a terrific battle, dispossessed He-ba-cha-ge. And now he had grown old in exile. His horns were worn down to two blunt stumps, and his skin was drawn into numerous wrinkles. His strength had failed him, but never his courage.

It happened that on the same day that He-ba-cha-ge sat dreaming in the heat of the sun, Sin-de-dum-pa, Stub-tail, the Grizzly, came out from among his hiding places to feed. It also happened that on this very day he chose for his feeding ground the same hill on which He-ba-cha-ge sat to sun himself and to dream of the days when he proudly lorded it over a goodly-sized herd to the exclusion of all other bulls. There being nothing to make him afraid, Sin-de-dum-pa sniffed among the bunches of grass, hooked a ground-apple [prairie turnip] out of the hard sod with his long claws, or stopped for a moment at the house of a family of red ants to put his moistened paw upon the swarm and then lick the acid emitted thereon by them. The chipmunks, the prairie-dogs, and the ground-squirrels hurriedly betook themselves to their holes when they saw Sin-de-dum-pa come along swaying his head from side to side in accompaniment to his heavy footsteps, and the birds took to their wings with frightened cries.

Suddenly, Sin-de-dum-pa came face to face with the horned slumberer, who, hearing the sound of footsteps near, opened his eyes wide and then deliberately shut them again.

"Out of my way!" growled Sin-de-dum-pa fiercely. "Out of my way, you wrinkled fool!"

He-ba-cha-ge did not move even a hair, showed not the slightest sign of fear, but went on with his dreaming and chewing.

Enraged at this show of indifference to fear, Sin-de-dum-pa flew at He-ba-cha-ge and, seizing him by the beard, shrieked, "You are the person who boasted to coyote and to badger that you do not fear me, that you could whip me. I dare you to do it, even now, upon this very ground!" and then gave him a fearful blow with his paw upon the face.

He-ba-cha-ge turned his face slowly to one side and muttered to himself, "Why don't you fight him? You were no mean fighter at one time!"

"What did you say!" snorted Sin-de-dum-pa. "You are insulting me, I know!"

"I did say something," replied He-ba-cha-ge, slowly rising to his feet. "I said, 'why don't you fight him,' and I am going to fight you!"

Surprised at the sudden awakening of courage in He-ba-cha-ge, Sin-de-dum-pa sprang up on his haunches, spread out his arms and claws, and showed his teeth.

Trembling with anger to the very tip of his tail, He-ba-cha-ge lowered his massive head, pawed the earth once or twice, then, breathing out a hissing sound, plunged forward. He struck his antagonist just below the ribs. With a mighty grunt Sin-de-dum-pa tumbled over. He sprang to his feet but was immediately tossed up into the air, then again and again like a great hairy ball. By some chance Sin-de-dum-pa touched ground, and then by plunging, rolling, and kicking he managed to escape his terrible opponent and dash into the thicket nearby.

After a time, when Sin-de-dum-pa had recovered his breath and nursed his bruises, he very cautiously peered over the tops of the bushes and beheld old He-ba-cha-ge quietly chewing and dozing as though nothing out of the way had happened. Bracing himself in readiness for flight should there be occasion to do so, Sin-de-dump-pa called in a frightened tone, "Hey! You, over there! We shall be friends henceforth, for we are equal in strength and courage!"

He-ba-cha-ge did not so much as turn his head but went on dreaming, perhaps of the days when he was young and was lord of a goodly-sized herd.

Kae-tun-ga on the War Path

This story is La Flesche's version of "How the Big Turtle Went on the War-Path." La Flesche had assisted in translating and interpreting the version of the story collected by Dorsey.

"I'M GOING ON THE WAR PATH," said Kae-tun-ga [big turtle] to a number of persons who had gathered at his teepee in answer to his call, "Who will go with me?"

"I will go with you!" exclaimed In-da-pa, the stone corn crusher, "and crush and bruise and smash the enemy."

"And I!" shouted Wa-ku, the awl, "and punch and pierce them with my sharp spear!"

"And I!" crackled Na-we-he, the firebrand, sending upward a sputter of sparks and a cloud of blue smoke, "and singe them and scorch them and make them sizzle and sozzle!"

And the war party, as did all war parties before them, marched in a procession around the camp circle and danced the coyote dance, a magic dance that made the warriors feel brave, and the enemy, far away, tremble with fear. Kae-tun-ga looked fine and brave as he danced and whirled about, mimicking the antics of the coyote, and the wide flaps of his deer-skin leggings flipped and flapped at every step, and the eagle feathers that adorned his lance fluttered gaily in the breeze. No less fine and brave did the others look as with loud war cries they danced around the camp circle following their valiant leader. And the men and the women and the children gathered about them to encourage them and to cheer them on.

When the coyote dance was over, the warriors proudly marched out of the camp in single file toward the land of the enemy, far away beyond the broad prairies and many wide and deep rivers. They were gone four days and four nights when all of a sudden they were met and stopped by Te-nu-ga, the buffalo bull who wished to join them.

"Oh! Brave warriors," he said. "Let me go with you and have a share in the spoils and honors of your expedition."

"You have a fine and commanding appearance," replied Kae-tun-ga, encouragingly, "but unless you show us what power there is in you that we can depend on to help us, we may not let you go with us. You see, here is In-da-pa, who can crush and bruise and smash the enemy, and there is Wa-ku, who can punch and pierce them with his sharp spear, and by his side stands Na-we-he, who can singe them and scorch them and make them sizzle and sozzle. Every one of them is an able warrior, and each one has the power to disable the enemy. Though your appearance is fine and commanding, it is not a sign to us that you have the qualities that make up a warrior."

"It will not be difficult to show you," answered Te-nu-ga, proudly, "that I am an able warrior, as able as any of your followers, and that I will show you right now and in this very place."

Te-nu-ga lowered his head and tossed up his little tail, trembling all over from the force and energy that was fast gathering within him. He pawed the earth angrily and darkened the sky with a thick cloud of dust, and he thrust his horns again and again into the ground and tore up the green sod, snorting and bellowing all the while with a rage and fury that sent the chipmunks and the gophers and the prairie dogs pellmell into their burrows in terror and the robins and the meadow larks and the swallows in full flight over the hills. Suddenly he plunged forward; his huge head came with a biff and a bang against the trunk of a dead oak that stood nearby all charred and scarred by many angry lightnings. The great tree quivered for a moment from the shock and then fell with a crash, scattering its broken limbs all over the ground.

Te-nu-ga wheeled about and looked expectantly toward the leader of the war party, but he simply turned his face away and said to his followers, "What a useless waste of force and energy. Come, my brave men, let us hasten to the land of the enemy and leave this great blusterer to himself."

The warriors moved on and for several days met with nothing unusual or any accident until they came to a wide and deep river. This retarded for a time their progress, but only for a short time, for out of his resourcefulness Kae-tun-ga built a raft upon which he placed his warriors, none of whom could swim, as well as all the baggage. He then jumped into the water and by swimming proceeded to tow the raft with its load across the stream. He had gone but a short distance when he heard behind him a hissing sound and an outcry by his warriors, "Na-we-he has fallen into the water and is drowned!"

Kae-tun-ga did not pause even for a moment but went on tugging away at the raft, and to cheer and comfort the rest of his men he said to them, "Be not discouraged at this mishap. In the struggles of war, accidents and death come to the aggressors as well as to the defenders, and so we must not let the death of one man dishearten us. We must keep straight on toward the land of our enemies. Na-we-he is dead, and we miss him, but there is solace in the thought that he died the death of a warrior, which is nobler than any other, and he is now with the spirit warriors whose home is in the clouds in the sky. His share of the honors we shall win in this enterprise will follow him there. We will stop for nothing, but go on till we reach the land of the enemy."

When the warriors landed on the other side, they found waiting for them Seen-ga the squirrel, who asked permission to join the war party. Knowing the worth of the applicant as a warrior, Kae-tun-ga accepted him without even so much as a challenge, and the war party moved on with eager haste.

In a few days after that, the warriors came to the camp of the enemy, and about midnight Kae-tun-ga, like an experienced warrior, proceeded to arrange his forces on the grounds which seemed to him the most advantageous. "Go," he said to Seen-ga, "and take your position in the tallest cottonwood tree you can find near the lake and watch until [I] call for you. Yours shall be the most important part in this attack." Seen-ga disappeared at a bound in the darkness and was off to take the position assigned to him.

"And you," said Kae-tun-ga to In-da-pa, "though deaf, dumb, and blind like your companion, you shall do your part as though you had eyes, ears, and the power of speech. You shall sit in the middle of the path that leads to the spring where the people go every day to get water. There you will meet the enemy at the proper time and do the damage to the foe that I expect you to do."

"And you," he said to Wa-ku, "my warrior of the sharp lance, shall lie in wait in the very midst of the camp in the well-beaten path that leads from house to house, in a place most conspicuous. There you shall meet the foe and thrust them with your sharp blade. I shall lie concealed among the ash heaps along the outskirts of the camp until the opportunity arises for me to attack."

Just before break of day a young woman came out of her teepee and hurried along the path toward the spring to get water. Her foot struck something hard, which she hastily picked up and examined. "Oh, what a beautiful crusher I have found for myself," she exclaimed. "I shall use it as soon as I get home."

When the young woman got home, she immediately got out a bag of corn and set to work to pound some of it into flour to make cakes. She hummed a tune as she worked and kept time to the rhythmic motions of her arms and hands. By a sudden mismove she brought the crusher down square upon her fingers. She uttered a cry of pain and threw the crusher rattling out of the door, exclaiming as she did so, "What a horrid, horrid crusher that is. I don't want it any more!"

At about sunrise another young woman came out of her teepee and walked rapidly along the path that led from house to house. Her eyes caught sight of the awl, and with a cry of pleasure she picked it up and said, "I shall hasten home and use the beautiful awl that I have found for myself." As soon as she got home she took out from her work bag a pair of unfinished moccasins and began to work. The awl worked very well until it suddenly slipped and pierced her finger through. She winced and uttered a little cry of pain and hurled the awl rattling out of the door, saying as she did so, "What a bad, bad awl that is to hurt my finger so; I am sorry I found it!"

At this very moment there arose a cry of alarm toward the outskirts of the camp, and then the people ran excitedly about the teepees shouting, "Kae-tun-ga the warrior is captured!" Soon they brought him to the middle of the camp kicking and struggling to free himself.

"Kill him, kill him!" shouted the people, all angry and excited. "Hit him with your stone axes!"

"How foolish these people are!" said Kae-tun-ga, having now ceased to struggle. "Don't you know that if you hit me with your stone axes, you will break your own legs and not hurt me a bit? The axes would glance against my hard back and break your shins that are not protected."

"That is true!" exclaimed the people. "Don't endanger the lives of the children, but throw him in the fire."

"That would be just as bad," said Kae-tun-ga. "I would struggle and kick violently, scattering the live coals in every direction and burn your children!"

"True, true!" exclaimed the people. "Then put him in boiling water!"

"Is there no end to your folly!" said Kae-tun-ga. "I would

struggle and kick and splash the boiling water all over your children and scald them. Then what would you do!"

Before another foolish suggestion was made for the destruction of the old warrior was offered, a thirsty little youngster cried to its mother, "Nee, nee, na-ha, nee!" ("Water, water, mother, water!")

Upon hearing this, Kae-tun-ga fell to the ground in a heap, trembling violently and groaning, "Ah, ah!"

"He's afraid of water!" shouted the people, all in one voice. "Take him to the lake and drown him!"

"He, he, ah, ah!" groaned Kae-tun-ga in terror as they dragged him kicking and struggling to the lake. When they reached the bank of the lake, two strong men seized the warrior by the wrists and ankles and swung him back and forth several times and then flung him far into the lake where it was the deepest. With a crash and a splash Kae-tun-ga fell into the water, and a great many little bubbles played upon the surface as he sank to the bottom.

"He's dead, he's dead!" yelled the people for very joy, but hardly had the echoes of their voices died away when a young man called out, "He's not dead at all. There he is, making faces at us!"

Sure enough, there he was, his head sticking out of the water, and he winked one eye and then the other at the people in an insulting manner. "Is there no end to the stupidity of these people!" he said. "Did you not know that water is my life and my home and that I am happiest when I am in the mud of a lake!" He then gently sank and disappeared, leaving a ring of ripples which was joined by another, each widening and becoming fainter until the surface of the lake became smooth and placid again.

"Bail the water out of the lake!" screamed the people in angry fury, and all went to work bailing the water with great vigor. The day passed and night came, but the lake was as deep as when they began. They were still standing on the bank all soaked and bespattered with mud when the dawn of the morrow came. Then they looked up and saw Pay-ton, the crane, flying overhead. With one voice they called to him to come and swallow the water of the lake for them. Pay-ton came down and, standing among the flags along the edge of the lake, began to drink. At each swallow the great bird gave a whoop that could be heard for the distance of many hills and valleys. The water of the lake began to go down, down, down, until the muddy back of Kae-tun-ga appeared above the surface. Then the people set up a shout of triumph and prepared to attack their enemy. Kae-tun-ga in a voice of despair called to his warrior stationed among the branches of a tall cottonwood tree near the lake. Uttering a loud war cry in response, Seen-ga sprang forward and, leaping from branch to branch and tree to tree, came directly over Pay-ton and pounced upon him from above and, swinging beneath him, cut a deep gash in his breast. The water rushed out, and the lake was once again filled.

Seeing that Pay-ton was dead and the lake filled again and Kae-tun-ga safe at the bottom, the people called loudly for Nu-shnon, the otter, who was as much at home under water as on land besides being a good warrior. Nu-shnon responded promptly and down he went to the bottom of the lake. It was not long before he found Kae-tun-ga and attacked him. After a short struggle Kae-tun-ga caught his antagonist by his left foot and held him fast. "I shall not let you go until I hear thunder!" said Kae-tun-ga. Then Nu-shnon called for help, but no one could go to his assistance. The people could hear the noise of the struggle going on in the water, they heard Kae-tun-ga say he would not let his prisoner go until thunder came, so they made large drums and pounded upon them. But the old warrior said, "Those are drums and not thunder. I shall know when thunder does come and not till then shall I let you go." And so Kae-tun-ga held Nu-shnon prisoner there under the lake all the long winter. Then at last spring came and with it the voice of thunder. Kae-tun-ga released his prisoner, and the war was over.

Kae-tun-ga gathered his warriors together and started on his homeward journey, satisfied with the victories he had won, and when he was approaching his home, he, with his braves, gathered grass and, piling it in a heap, set fire to it as a signal to their friends at home that they were coming. When the people of the village saw the black smoke rising skyward, they hastened in a mass over the hills to meet the returning warriors. With noisy shouts of victory the people carried their braves into the village, and all that day and night they danced the dance of triumph led by the brave old warrior. As when Kae-tun-ga danced the coyote dance before he marched against his enemies, the wide flaps of his fine buckskin leggings flipped and flapped at every step of the dance of triumph, and when the dance was over, there the tale ended.

Part Three

*Stories of the Recent Past
and the Reservation*

A Ghost Story

During his youth Francis La Flesche heard many ghost stories, which were common among the Omahas, and told both Ponca and Dakota ghost stories to Dorsey. The story that follows broadly parallels his "Ponka Ghost Story," in which Poncas on the warpath follow a voice to the foot of a tree, where they find the bones of a Dakota that had fallen when the platform on which the body had rested had collapsed. The episode takes place after flintlocks were introduced into Omaha culture during the first quarter of the nineteenth century.

"YES," SAID PA-SEE-DU-BA IN answer to a question. "We were camped down in the timber along the Missouri River. It was in the fall of the year when the leaves of the trees were turning yellow. The deer in the vicinity of the camp had been about killed off or scared away, so it was difficult to get fresh meat. Food in my house was getting scarce, so it became necessary for me to go out to find game. I went far up the river and crossed over to a place where hunters had not been. I scared up several deer but had no chance to shoot until late in the afternoon when a large buck jumped up from the tall grass. It suddenly stopped when it had gone several paces and turned to look at me. I took aim without dismounting and just [as] I pulled the trigger my horse moved and the ball struck the deer in the hind leg, breaking it. I dismounted and hobbled the horse and started on foot to pursue the wounded deer. There were plenty of other deer, but I was determined to get the one I had wounded, so I gave no attention to them. The sun was just going down when I overtook the wounded buck near the river. I shot it and looked about for a good camping place, carrying the deer with me, as I was far away from my horse and it would have been difficult to find it in the dark.

The sun had gone down, and it was just dark enough so that you could not recognize a face, when I came to a bend of the river where the red willows and young cottonwood trees grew thick. This was just a short distance from the place where Sioux City now stands but was at a time when there were no white people in this part of the country. As I pushed my way through the young trees, I came to a cluster of hard willows, the tops of which were gathered together and bent over by the weight of heavy grape vines. It formed a natural shelter against wind and rain, and it would conceal me from war parties that might be passing by; I had nothing else to fear. With a sense of relief I threw down the deer and trampled down the weeds that grew under the vines and willows, and kneeling down I took from my hunting pouch my steel, flint, and punk and struck a spark. Soon the flames from my camp fire were cheerily leaping upward, and I set to work dressing the deer. There was no moon, but the stars shone brightly and scarcely a breeze stirred the leaves about me. The night was so quiet that the least noise I made sounded loud and distinct.

"I finished dressing the deer, and being very hungry, I took the liver and spread it over the live coals to broil. I was just in the act of turning the meat over when all of a sudden I heard the shout of a man, loud and clear. The voice was that of a young man, but there was something in it that was strange and undefinable, and it sent through me a thrill of fear unlike the fear that arises from the meeting of a living natural enemy. I hastily smothered the flames by scattering the burning wood with my feet, and then, grasping my gun, I pressed myself back into the branches of the willows and the grape vines where it was dark, and I waited. Soon there came sounds of footsteps. I could hear plainly the cracking of the dead willow saplings at each step and the snapping of the young trees against a buffalo robe. The sounds came nearer and nearer until they came close up to my hiding place, and then at that very moment, a piece of dead willow wood rolled over from the fireplace and with a crackling sound sent up some lively sparks and then burst into flame.

Then in the glare of the light there stood before me a figure that would have sent me to my death from very fear had I not already recovered from the first shock of fright. Its matted hair hung loosely over the shoulders, and the skin of the top of its head was in some way torn off, leaving the bone exposed. The skin of its face was black and shriveled, and its teeth protruded from its lipless mouth; from its neck down to its knees its body was encased in rawhide. Its arms of bones dangled from its shoulders as it stood there on its legs and feet of bones. It peered into the flame with its eyeless sockets, swaying its head from side to side. It seemed to ignore my presence. The muzzle of my gun — a flintlock — which was charged with a handful of powder and a ball about the size of a hickory nut, almost touched its side. It bent over to reach its bony hand into the flame when I pulled the trigger. The pan flashed with a hissing sound. An explosion followed which roared through the valley and the hills. The ball tore a hole through the rawhide casing almost as big as my fist. The flame went out, a sound like a heavy sigh arose, and a gust of wind whirled the grape vine over my head round and round, and the thing had vanished. All sense of fear left me and I quietly rekindled my fire, carefully searched for the meat I had put on the coals to broil, and it was gone.

"I arose very early in the morning and, carrying on my back the meat and skin, pushed my way through the red willows toward the open prairie toward my horse. As I plodded along, I wondered if the happening of the night before was real or only a vision arising in a mind upset by thoughts of the lonely surroundings and of unseen dangers. I came to the open and began laboriously to climb a hill, for the meat was heavy and I bent forward. A low oak tree with wide-spreading limbs stood on the side of the hill near the top. I was about to pass it when I saw through the corner of my eye something white. I looked up and there, leaning up against the trunk of the tree, stood my visitor of the night before, exactly as I had seen him. He stood there with his head partly twisted aside. Around him on the ground were strewn locks of his hair and bits of skin which had rotted and fallen from his casing of rawhide. Among the limbs of the tree were some poles arranged as for a platform. Some had dropped to the ground and lay scattered about his feet. I stood for a while looking at this man that walked in his endless sleep and then went on my way, still wondering if it were all real or only a vision.

Hal Baker

In the early 1880s, officials of the Indian Office experimented with a policy of leasing reservation lands to cattlemen. The policy was soon abandoned for a number of reasons. Foremost, perhaps, was that cattlemen obtained leases at notoriously low costs. In addition, white reformers who sought assimilation of the Indians argued that money derived from leases gave the Indians less incentive to work and that the cattlemen who had leases opposed the opening of Indian lands in order to protect their own interests. In this story, set on an unnamed reservation, perhaps in the early 1880s, La Flesche subtly probes the corruption that attended the leasing system and the argument by American entrepreneurs that the Indians were not "using" the land, an argument that later became a part of the rationale for allotting lands and opening surplus reservation lands to non-Indian settlement.

O NE MORNING THE MAJOR SAT at his desk in the little office busily figuring on scraps of paper. At times he would drop his pen and sit motionless, gazing at the blank wall in thoughtful contemplation, unmindful of all that was going on in the room and outside. Since he took charge of affairs at the agency and had started the office work according to his own ideas, he had driven all over the eastern part of the reservation to study its resources. Much as he was impressed with the richness of the land and its possibilities in the way of agriculture, he had quickly abandoned all the plans that suggested themselves to his mind for its development when he drove through the great forest among the hills along the river. A new interest had arisen. His mind became alert and active when he beheld trees whose immense trunks stood from twenty to thirty feet in height with scarcely a branch or knot to mar their beauty. There were black walnut, white oak, ash, and other hardwood trees with whose commercial value he was thoroughly familiar. He measured the girth of one and with a practiced eye estimated its height and figured out its value in money with consummate accuracy. Years of active work in the lumber business, an enterprise in which he finally failed and lost all the wealth he had accumulated, had given him a training in the measurement of timber that was amazingly unerring. Here was wealth incalculable. Although most of the finest trees grew on steep hillsides or in deep ravines difficult of access, he was not at all dismayed, for he was as good an engineer as he was a lumberman, and he could build roads among the trees on the hillsides or in the ravines. He would dig for these riches as the miner digs for the gold or other precious metals that make the standard wealth of a commercial people. He had made a hasty survey of the grounds where he could build his roads to reach the trees most desirable.

It was with these things that his mind was preoccupied as he sat at his desk in the little office taking no notice of his surroundings. Once more the Major laid aside his pen and leaned back in his chair to take another mental view of his discovery and to make his calculations, when suddenly he was aroused by a loud cry outside, "Hey—o! Hey—o!" followed by the loud cracking of whips and the clattering of many hoofs and horns. "Head them off there to the right; don't crowd them too close. Hey—o! Hey—o! Crack, crack!"

"What's all that noise, John?" asked the Major, turning with a disturbed expression to the clerk who sat at another desk, struggling to balance his cash accounts. "Can't it be stopped?"

"Why, Major, that is Hal Baker, the cattleman," replied the clerk, with his pen poised in the air. "The grazing season is over, and he is driving his herd to winter quarters just outside the reservation. I think he will come in presently as he usually does."

The last word was hardly uttered when there came a vigorous rap at the door, and before there was an answer it flew wide open and in walked the cattleman, his big spurs clanking at each step. His was a figure that at once attracted attention and inspired admiration, whether sitting, walking, or riding. Tall and handsome, he was well proportioned, with ruddy complexion, pinkish eyelids, and a heavy blond turned-up mustache. Without the least hesitation he strode with a confident air to the Major's desk, and removing his broad-brimmed brown hat with a sweeping motion of the arm, he said, "This, I presume, is Major Moore of whom I have heard so much of late. My name is Baker, Hal Baker." And he took the Major's proffered hand, giving it such a hearty squeeze and shake that it made him spring on his toes and wince. Then the cattleman turned to the clerk, gave him a nod of recognition and the slyest kind of a wink, the meaning of which that individual seemed to have well understood, for, mumbling some sort of an excuse, he tip-toed to the door and disappeared.

"Well," said the Major, after he had measured with his eyes the form of the visitor as though he were to be cut into inch boards, "Mr. Baker, will you be seated, and will you tell me something about your business. They tell me that you are grazing cattle on the reservation. How many have you, may I ask?"

"Something like five thousand head, Major," promptly replied the cattleman. "This is a new enterprise to me and has been successful so far. By careful management I hope to make enough money out of it before very long and retire so as to give the next fellow a chance. It's a risky business, Major. In the summertime it is well enough, although sometimes there is great loss from lump-jaw and the hoof-disease, but the thing most dreaded by cattlemen of the west is the awful blizzard. Being an eastern man, Major, I suppose you have never seen one; you will by next January. I hope you have a very heavy fur overcoat; you will need it. I tell you, when the cattle begin to draw their tails between their hind legs and hump their backs, they are freezing, and the owner, if he is any sort of a man, will go among them and yell 'Hey — o! Hey — o!' and make them move about lively until they get warm again. Many's the night I've had to go out with a lantern to save my cattle that way. When the wind is sweeping everything and the snow is so thick you can't see further than the length of your arm. A man who likes to sit by the kitchen stove and watch his wife fry bacon had better keep out of the cattle business, that's what I think."

"Of course, Mr. Baker," said the Major, "you have made some sort of business arrangement with the Agent or the Indians themselves for the use of the land, or grazing privilege; would you mind telling me what it is?"

"Why," replied Hal Baker, "I made an agreement with the chiefs that for the grazing of five thousand head of cattle I give at the end of every season twenty head of steers, or earlier if they should demand them and — "

"But," broke in the Major, "it seems to me that twenty head of steers valued, let us say, at forty dollars a head at the most, would hardly be an adequate compen — "

"The adequacy of the compensation," interrupted the cattleman, "has never been questioned by the chiefs, and they have always received the steers gladly and without complaint. I deliver them promptly at the time agreed upon or whenever demanded. Nobody is robbed, Major, and many besides the Indians are benefited by the use of a little of the thousands and thousands of tons of wild grass that annually goes to waste or is burnt up by the fires that sweep over the prairies every fall. I tell you a prairie fire is a wonderful sight at night and in the daytime too, but, Major, it is wonderfully destructive, too. Back in Virginia, where you come from, you never see one. You will see them before long, and you will agree with me that the grass my cattle eat is but very little as compared with the amount that goes to ashes. And just think, the Indians get their twenty fat steers without doing a lick of work to earn them, have a glorious feast and a tomahawk dance, and are happy. With a great deal of labor I fatten the cattle through the winter, then ship them to Kansas City, Chicago, New York, or any place where I can get the best price for them. The meat feeds many hungry mouths, and the hides are put to use in a great variety of ways. Why, if I or somebody else did not come and utilize a little of this rich grass, nobody would get any good out of it."

As he sat talking with his chair tipped back and rocking backward and forward, Hal Baker took out of his pocket five twenty-dollar gold pieces and toyed with them on the corner of the Major's desk, arranging them now in a row, and then piling them up one on top of the other. Suddenly he arose, saying: "Well, Major, I'll have to hurry along if I want to get home before night with my little herd. I shall be passing by here again before long, and we will have another talk. Perhaps we can find some way of helping our dusky brethren here toward a better way of living, although they seem to be perfectly contented to live in their own simple way. Good-bye, sir. If I can be of any service to you, all you've got to do is just to say so." He gave the Major another painful squeeze of the hand, clanked through the length of the room to the door, and out.

The Major dropped wearily into his chair, drew a long breath, tipped his chair back, clasping his hands against the back of his head as he did so, and tried to pick up the thread of his thought where he had left it when Hal Baker came in. But the glimmer of some metallic object on the corner of the desk caught his eyes and down came the front of his chair; he rested one elbow on the edge of the desk and stared hard at the stack of gold coins. He took a stealthy glance at the door, then at each of the windows, and then his hand slyly slid toward the yellow pile. He grasped it; he slowly counted the pieces and dropped them one by one into his pocket. Just then the door suddenly swung open. The Major gave a start, and the cattleman walked in.

"I'm sorry to interrupt you again, Major," he apologized, "but I'm always forgetting this old whip," reaching under the desk. "Didn't think of it till I got down to the road. Well, good-bye again."

Down at the end of the road Hal Baker met the clerk, who called out to him, "Well, Hal, did he bite?"

"Never saw one that didn't," replied the cattleman, "and here's the key to your safe," throwing something round and shiny to the clerk.

John deftly caught the object, tossed it in the air, and caught it again as it came down and thrust it into his pocket, saying, "I say, Hal, you're a good 'un."

Ne-ma-ha

Robert Merriman, the central character in this story, appears as Robert Redwing or Philip Redwing in a number of fragments of stories among La Flesche's papers in the Smithsonian Institution. This story, like the fragments, confronts the issue of assimilation. The process, however, is not the result of policy decisions in Washington, but of abandonment. In his despair, Ne-ma-ha attempts the rite called $no^{n'}zhi^{n}zho^{n}$, in which a youth, in four days of fasting, prayed to $Wako^{n'}da$ for help through life. Though he has heard about it only in stories, in desperation he sings the song of supplication, but there is no response. Ne-ma-ha is taken away before he can absorb the customs and be initiated into the practice of his culture. Thus the end of the story leaves the reader with a question: What lies ahead for the central character, who has rediscovered his tribal ties after so many years among the whites?

I

"AWAY! OUT OF MY SIGHT! I wish never to see you again!" exclaimed a tall, fierce-looking man as he violently pushed a boy from him.

The angry voice rose above the rattling of tent poles and the bustle of the people who were busy breaking camp. Startled by this outburst of anger, those nearby paused in their work to see what was the matter, and as they beheld the boy gather up his little robe and bow and walk slowly out of camp with quivering lips and bowed head, they were moved to pity. A murmur of

118

disapproval spread on all sides, but no open protest was made, for the quarrelsome disposition of the man was well known; even the mother, who felt keenly the distress of her child, dared not so much as lift her eyes in reproach.

The lad climbed the nearest hill; reaching the top, he threw himself prone to the ground and wept as though his heart would break. Already the caravan was fording the river below with all the excitement usual in crossing a stream. The mother was the last to move, although she had been among the first in readiness. As she took the trail, leading her horses, she looked back from time to time as though expecting to see her child following. When he had overcome the first paroxysms of grief, the boy sat up and looked across the river toward the opposite bluffs. There was but one person ascending the rise; all the rest had gone beyond. Although the figure looked small and dim in the distance, the lad recognized his mother, and the thought that she had stopped once more to look for him started afresh the sobs and tears. At last she turned and moved on, and he watched her longingly until she slowly disappeared behind the hills.

An oppressive stillness pervaded the deserted camp over which passed gusts of wind, carrying with them the ashes of dead fires in funnel-shaped clouds. Abandoned now by all the human associates upon which he had unconsciously depended for protection and comfort, the lad cast his eyes about as though seeking for aid from some unknown source. Far off against the green hills he saw groups of buffalo, elk, and antelope scattered here and there; above him in the blue sky great birds were soaring in wide circles, and below him the winding river shimmered in the sun. All these objects, which hitherto he had scarcely heeded, now arrested his attention and awakened within him a hope that some of them might take pity on him and bring him help. In the midst of nature's silence the lonely boy remembered the stories told of men, who, when mere lads and bereft of father and mother, had wandered over the prairies, where in solitude they had cried to Wa-kon-da for help, and their prayers had been heard and answered. Why should not I, he thought, pray to Wa-kon-da; perhaps my cry will be heard and answered. While this thought was still in his mind, the lad removed his moccasins, leggings, and robe and hid them in a bush close by; then returning to the top of the hill, he put moistened earth upon his face and head, and in a voice tremulous with emotion he cried to Wa-kon-da, using the song and words his mother had taught him.[1]

Wa-kon-da the-thu wa-pa-thin a - ton-he, Wa-kon-da the-thu wa-pa-thin a - ton-he.

He lifted his little hands to the sky, then brought them down to the earth, then he stretched them to the north, east, south, and west, the paths of the winds, as with tears streaming down his face he chanted his prayer. No suppliant before "the great spirit" was ever more in earnest. Again and again he offered his prayer, but there came no response. The sun steadily took its course, the waters of the river rippled on, and the wind sighed as before. At last the boy fell to the ground exhausted, and soon he was overcome with sleep.

The day was far spent when the lad was aroused by a mysterious consciousness of the presence near him of some living thing. Slowly and cautiously he lifted his head when lo! he beheld standing before him two strange bearded men, leaning on their guns and looking down upon him with pale eyes that gleamed under heavy brows and lashes. To spring up and run was the boy's first impulse, but at the same moment there flashed through his mind the thought that this vision might be an answer to his prayer, and he hesitated. The two men, wishing not to frighten the lad, moved toward the river and beckoned him to follow. He rose and silently pointed to the place where he had hidden his clothing, and, there being no signs of objection from the men to his getting them, the lad stepped to the bush, dressed himself, and followed the strangers.

II

On the morning following the banishment of the boy, the people again broke camp. Like a great serpent the caravan moved over the rolling prairie, leaving behind a dark, winding trail. Not a cloud broke the deep blue above, and the sun shed a glaring light upon the grassy hills. Toward the middle of the day a dark spot appeared in the western sky, and as though by magic other patches of clouds came to view. No notice was taken of these until a tall man with long hair looked up and exclaimed: "Ah ho! See what is going on above!"

The clouds moved swiftly around and around, then gathered in one surging mass. With lurid glare a bolt shot to the earth, followed by a roar that made the ground tremble, and smoke curled upward from the spot where the lightning had struck. Straight toward the caravan the cloud swept on with increasing speed; another fiery dart pierced the earth, and smoke arose as before. On came the cloud, making a noise like many wings; a third shot fell, and the tall man shouted, "Look out for the fourth!" The cloud was now overhead, rolling in angry turmoil. Great drops of rain fell slantwise, sparkling in the sun. The last word was still upon the lips of the tall man when there came a blinding flame with a terrific crash. The people fled in every direction, and a man sank to the ground enveloped in smoke. The cloud rushed on, leaving behind the sky calm and blue.

"Ho! They have killed one of us!" cried a voice loud and clear. The word passed swiftly on to the end of the line, and the people hurried to the spot where the man lay. No one dared to touch the body, for violent hands had been laid upon it by the thunder gods. One of the chiefs approached, and an opening was made for him. He walked to the prostrate form and, without touching it, examined it closely. Then turning to the people, he said, "Let this be a warning to men who treat their children cruelly. You all know what this man did but yesterday. To all appearances he is dead, but life may yet be lingering. Make haste and bring water, men, women, and children, and let there be a continuous flow upon the body."

Back and forth the people ran to a brook nearby, and they kept a constant stream of water upon the body. After a while there was a slight movement of the arms, then of the legs, and at last the man raised himself to a sitting position. The chief stepped forward and supported him. "I am alive," gasped the man, "but—I cannot see!" As the people looked at him, they saw, burnt around each eye, a black ring.

III

In the afternoon of a spring day as the shadows were lengthening, Mr. John Merriman, of the firm of Merriman, Primeaux and Company, dealers in furs and general merchandise, sat on the front veranda of his cottage in the residence part of the city of New Orleans. The roses and blossoming vines that twined over the windows and trellises, the garden with its variety of trees, flowers, and well-kept walks indicated the thrift of the people who dwelt there. Mrs. Merriman sat near her husband, gently rocking backward and forward as her deft fingers played rapidly over her work. Suddenly, she dropped her sewing and, shifting her chair so as to face her husband, said, "Do you think it is best for the boy to go so far away from home? He is young to take all that responsibility; I am afraid it will be too much for him."

"It will be the best thing in the world," replied Mr. Merriman, removing his pipe, "not only for him, but for the firm as well. He is better fitted for the place than any of the men we have, and besides, he will get double the salary he is now paid. Of course, we do not know his exact age. It's twenty years now since Primeaux and I found him, and at that time I think he was about eight. He'll get along all right."

"When did you hear of Krebs' death? How did it happen?"

"The news was brought last week by the steamboat. No details were given, but I don't think it was an accident. My judgement is that someone who was jealous of his success in the management of our business with the Indians killed him."

"Aren't you afraid that Robert might be killed in the same way?"

"There is no danger; the people who are suspected of killing Krebs have left the country and are not likely to return. What's more, Bob is an Indian, and the tribe will protect him."

"Does Robert think that he is going to his own people?"

"Bob doesn't know who his people are, doesn't even know their tribal name. He only remembers his own name and those of his father and mother."

There was a click at the gate, and the couple looked up. A tall, swarthy young man strode rapidly up the gravel walk. "Hello! Father," he called. "How is your knee?"

"It's there; so is that infernal rheumatism," answered Mr. Merriman, shifting his leg, which rested upon a pillow in a chair. "How is my boy?"

"I'm all right," said Robert, for it was he. "Only, I'm sorry I have to go so soon. I wish your knee was well; I don't like to see you suffer."

"Old age, my boy, old age," replied Mr. Merriman, grasping Robert's hand. "Aches and pains are the companions of old age. If the pain wasn't in my knee, it would be in some other part of my old body."

"Margy was here this morning," broke in Mrs. Merriman, as she dusted Robert's shoulders with her handkerchief, "and she feels dreadful about your going."

"I'll go and see her after supper."

"What time does the steamboat leave?"

"Two o'clock tomorrow afternoon."

IV

On his arrival at the trading post, Robert Merriman lost no time in examining the books, making an inventory of the stock, and soon had everything in working order. The men connected with the establishment quickly recognized the ability of the young man and accorded him the respect that they had shown to Krebs, the former agent.

No one really knew who Robert was. The employees, who had heard of the principals of the firm, whispered among themselves that he was a son of "old Merriman" by an Osage woman. The Indians took him for a young Spaniard, and they fell to calling him "Little Es-pa-yu-na."

When Robert had every branch of the business well in hand, he gave personal attention to his customers, frequently waiting upon them himself that he might become acquainted with every face and name. It did not satisfy him to deal with the Indians through an interpreter, and he set to work to learn the language. The words sounded strangely familiar to him as he repeated them, and the rapidity with which he learned to speak surprised the Indians.

Business thrived, and nothing unusual occurred until one day there came to the store an old woman leading a blind man. Robert waited upon them, and from the terms they used when addressing each other he learned that they were husband and wife. There was something familiar in their faces and in the tones of their voices. He was almost certain that he had seen the couple before but was puzzled by the disfigurement of the old man's face. The wife tied her purchases in a bundle, threw it over her back, and led her husband out of the store. Robert stood watching them and called to the interpreter, "Mack, who is the blind man who just went out with his wife? Seems to me I have seen them somewhere, but I can't remember."

"This first time you seen them," replied Mack. "That's Num′-pa-be. He's pretty bad man."

Robert gave a start as he heard the name. It was that of his father, which he had always remembered. "What is his wife's name?" he hurriedly asked.

"Ne′-da-we."

It was the name of his mother. Suddenly memories of the past long dormant swept through his mind — the scene of his banishment, the strange bearded men who surprised him, and all that happened to him since that event. He strove to recall the features of his mother and father as he saw them when a child and to trace them in the faces he just looked upon, but the scars on the old man's face perplexed him. At last he asked, "Why do you say the old man is a bad man?"

"Long time ago," answered Mack, "that old man had one boy, his name, Ne-ma-ha."

"Go on," urged Robert as he heard his own name.

"I was goin' tell you. I use t' play with that boy when I was little. One time we went buffalo hunt, and the old man hit that boy and scare him away, and he never come back again. Next day lightning hit him and pretty near kill him. He's bad man; nobody like him."

Robert now realized that he was among his own people, that his father and mother were living, and he had seen them both. In the rush of feeling he could scarcely restrain his desire to run out, overtake, and embrace his mother, but the thought that he might be unwelcome to his father made him hesitate.

Leaving the store, he sought a place where he could be alone. His thoughts went back to his home and his adopted parents, whom he dearly loved. He put his hand mechanically to a pocket, slowly drew from it a letter received only a few days before this discovery, and opened it. His eyes fell upon the closing paragraph, and he read: "I helped your mother fix up your room today. We rearranged all the pictures and the curtains. Your little bow still hangs over the door. We are all looking anxiously toward the time when we shall see you again. I send you some roses I plucked from your window. Affectionately, Margaret." He returned the letter to its place, thinking that surely it would be right for him to devote the rest of his life to these people who loved and trusted him; yet he felt the promptings of a natural duty toward his real parents so lately discovered.

In the afternoon of the following day, Robert was standing at his desk working over his books when two Indians entered the store. After an exchange of greetings the men sat down upon a long bench kept for the use of customers, and one of them took from his belt his tobacco bag and filled his pipe. As he offered the pipe to his friend to light and to take the first whiffs, he said, "The old man died about the middle of the night, they say, and his wife was all alone with him."

Robert's quick ear caught the words and as he reached to dip his pen, he asked, "Who was that, Uncle?"

"Num'-pa-be, the blind man. Perhaps you know him."

As he heard the name, Robert's pen slipped from his hand and rolled over the neatly written page, leaving a trail of dark blotches. Without heeding the accident, he asked, "When will they bury him?"

"They have already buried him. It was a sad ending, they say," continued the man, turning to his friend. "Toward the last he kept saying, 'I heard his voice. I heard his voice.' "

Robert stood in silence a few moments, then stole softly out of the building and walked slowly away. Halfway up a hill he came to a solitary tree and sat down, leaning against its trunk. The shadows were fast deepening. Dusk came and then the darkness of night. As he sat going over the long years of loneliness and suffering through which his father must have passed, there crept into the mind of the young man a fear that he might have been to blame for it all. A feeling of self-reproach came over him; then, as though to ease his conscience, he welcomed the thought that when he lifted his little hands to "the great spirit" for aid, he was thinking only of his own misery and desolation and that he did not even for a moment desire the punishment of his father. Suddenly, he remembered his mother and hastily made his way toward the village.

The hour of midnight had passed. On a high hill overlooking the Indian lodges a bright fire was burning. By its side stood a woman watching; it was the faithful widow lighting the path for her husband to the land of spirits. Wearily, she shaded her face with one hand and looked up at the stars of Wa'-ba-ha (Ursa Major). "It has almost completed its circuit," she murmured.

"Day will soon come." She stooped to feed the fire once more; a sound caught her ear, and Robert stepped into the light.

Along the horizon a grey streak appeared; gradually, it took on a faint tinge of red; then quickly the whole eastern sky burst into a flame of crimson. With the glow upon his face, Robert said, "Mother, day has come," and taking her tenderly by the hand, he led her slowly down the hill, and the two vanished in the rising mist below.

NOTE

1. La Flesche attached the following note to the song: "Wa-kon-da here in need I stand."

Marion, the Book Vendor, and I

During his tenure as an employee of the Bureau of Indian Affairs, La Flesche took his annual vacation leave in the summer. In most years he returned home to Nebraska to visit relatives and friends, riding the train from Washington, D.C., to Bancroft, by way of Omaha, and then traveling the rest of the way by buggy or hack. The following story was probably based on an experience during one of his trips home.

A FTER A TEDIOUS WAIT BETWEEN trains in the city of Omaha, I strolled toward the depot, purchased my ticket, rechecked my baggage, and followed the hurrying crowd into the passenger car. I managed to secure a seat on the shady side of the coach, and having deposited my hand luggage and umbrella in one of the racks overhead, I settled down to read a magazine, the cover of which blazed with a picture in exaggerated coloring.

The belated passengers trod upon each other's heels as they pushed forward in their eagerness to get the most comfortable of the remaining seats. The car was nearly full when a woman entered, carrying in her arms two fretting children while a flaxen-haired boy of some seven or eight years followed, clinging to the skirt of her dress. At the middle of the car the mother paused with her brood and looked helplessly around. The conductor, seeing the embarrassment of the woman, stepped forward, removed a number of satchels and packages from a seat put there to preempt a place, and motioned her to sit down. The woman and the two children filled the space, and there was no room for the boy; the conductor moved toward me, I shifted my position, and the youngster took his place by my side.

There was a clanging of a bell, a hissing of steam, a series of quick, loud puffs at the engine, and the train moved slowly out of the station, gradually increasing its speed. My companion sat perfectly still, keeping a steady gaze upon the picture on my magazine, although his face, like those of the rest of the passengers, was streaming with perspiration, and the corners of his eyes were filled with cinders.

We had rattled on for a mile or so when a book vendor entered and made his way down the aisle, leaning over this person and that one, whispering confidentially to each of the latest, best, and cheapest novels. Some took a glance at the books, and others waved the man aside, but he moved on without the slightest change of expression on his face. He came to my seat, bent over my silent companion, and said to me, "I know you need a book to read on your long journey. It serves to pass away the time and breaks the monotony of travel. Now, here's a book that you ought to read. It is the latest and the cheap—"

"Oh! It's too hot for books!" I broke in, mopping my face.

"It ain't too hot for that thing you're reading!" he rejoined as he passed on.

My companion sat motionless as a sphinx, staring with wide, blue eyes at the tip of his toe, which he had now braced against the back of the seat in our front.

The uniformed book vendor again appeared, but instead of the shabby, paper-covered books, he carried upon his arm a large basket, and the burden of his speech, as he glanced to the right and to the left, was upon the cheapness of his bananas and the freshness of the peaches and pears. There was no more eagerness among the passengers for the fruit than there had been for the books, but the man moved slowly on, now and again clutching at the tops of the seats to steady himself as the car swayed from side to side.

Perhaps there was no need of sympathy for the vendor of books and fruit, yet as I noticed the apparent lack of success in his business, a friendly feeling for him arose within me which I could not resist. Again he learned toward me over the flaxen-headed boy, but before his oft-repeated words had left his lips, I asked, "How much are your pears?"

"These are three for ten, and these here are one for a nickel; which will you have?"

"I think I'll take a nickel one."

"All right," replied the man, with the same spiritless expression on his face. "They're mighty good pears."

As I felt about in my pocket for a nickel, the fruit vendor made a selection for me; my eye was on the very pear he picked up, as it had upon it a large spot which was a mute contradiction to the statement that it was fresh. The man deftly turned the spot side of the fruit to the palm of his hand, and holding it toward me rosy side up, he repeated the words "mighty good pears!" took his nickel, and walked on.

There was a movement at my side. I turned, and my little

companion looked up in my face. "I never had none o' them," he said in a drawling tone, glancing at the uplifted pear. "Down in Ohio we had one tree, but it never had none o' them."

"You lived in Ohio, did you?"

"Yes, we live in Nebraska now. Me and my mother been down to Kansas. She thought we would be home in one day, but we've been on the road a day and a half now."

"What is your name?"

"Marion."

"When did you leave Ohio?"

"We've been out here almost two years now. We sold the old place 'cause we thought we could get more land out here and raise all the apples and peaches and corn that we want." Turning another glance upon the pear, he again said, "I never had none o' them."

I took my penknife and cut the coveted fruit across the middle, carefully avoiding the decayed spot, and gave him the pointed half. Without another word he put it to his mouth; there was a gurgling sound, a smacking of lips, and he held the little black stem up to me and said, "Throw that out of the window, will you?"

I complied with the request, and the flaxen-haired urchin, having bettered his condition, doubled up his little legs upon the cushioned seat and was soon fast asleep.

We clattered on 'mid smoke, cinders, dust, and heat. We swiftly passed great fields of corn, wheat, and other grain, and wide pastures in which hundreds of cattle were grazing. Suddenly, the train slackened speed, and the engine shrieked long and loud; the conductor threw open the door and called out, "Bancroft! All out for Bancroft."

The mother arose, gathered up the two sleeping infants, gave me an appealing look, and then tottered toward the door. I shook my companion, lifted him to his feet, and he followed his mother, rubbing his eyes as he went. I too walked out; the train moved on, and we three, Marion, the book vendor, and I, went our several ways.